Table of Contents

Introduction

What are the new Common Core assessments?

The Common Core State Standards for English Language Arts have set shared, consistent, and clear objectives of what students are expected to learn. The standards are intended to be rigorous and reflect what students will need to be able to do to be college and career ready by the end of high school.

As a part of this initiative, two consortia of states, the Partnership for Assessment of Readiness for College and Careers (PARCC) and Smarter Balanced, have developed new assessments that are aligned with the Common Core State Standards and designed to measure students' progress toward college and career readiness.

How are the new assessments different?

The new standardized assessments from both PARCC and Smarter Balanced are designed to be taken online and include many new types of assessment items.

In addition to multiple-choice questions, the assessments include both short and extended constructed-response questions, which require students to develop written responses that include examples and details from the text.

Another key element in the PARCC and Smarter Balanced assessments is the two-part question. In two-part questions, Part B asks students to identify the text evidence that supports their answer to Part A. These questions reflect the new emphasis on text evidence in the Common Core Standards. Anchor Standard 1 states that students should "cite specific textual evidence when writing or speaking to support conclusions drawn from the text."

The assessments from PARCC and Smarter Balanced also include technology-enhanced questions. These items, which students will encounter if they take the online assessments, ask students to interact with and manipulate text. For example, some questions ask students to select two or three correct answers from a list. Other questions ask students to identify important events in a story and then arrange them in the correct order.

Newmark LEARNING
4
Common Core

Reading
Warm-Ups & Test Practice

Newmark Learning
629 Fifth Avenue, Pelham, NY • 10803

Editor: Ellen Ungaro
Designer: Raquel Hernández

Photo credits: Page 96: North Wind Picture Archives/Alamy

The assessments from PARCC and Smarter Balanced will also feature passages that meet the requirements for complex texts set by the Common Core State Standards. The ability to read and comprehend complex text is another key element of the new standards. Anchor Standard 10 for reading states that students should be able to "Read and comprehend complex literary and informational texts independently and proficiently."

Common Core Reading Warm-Ups and Test Practice is designed to help prepare students for these new assessments from PARCC and Smarter Balanced. The Warm Ups and Practice Tests will help students rehearse the kind of thinking needed for success on the online assessments.

What Test Will Your State Take?

Smarter Balanced States	PARCC States
Alaska	Arizona
California	Arkansas
Connecticut	Colorado
Delaware	District of Columbia
Hawaii	Florida
Idaho	Georgia
Iowa	Illinois
Kansas	Indiana
Maine	Kentucky
Michigan	Louisiana
Missouri	Maryland
Montana	Massachusetts
Nevada	Mississippi
New Hampshire	New Jersey
North Carolina	New Mexico
North Dakota	New York
Oregon	North Dakota
Pennsylvania	Ohio
South Carolina	Oklahoma
South Dakota	Pennsylvania
U.S. Virgin Islands	Rhode Island
Vermont	Tennessee
Washington	
West Virginia	
Wisconsin	
Wyoming	

How will this book help my students prepare for the new assessments?

Warm Ups for Guided Practice

Common Core Reading Warm-Ups & Test Practice includes ten Warm Up tests that are designed to provide students with an opportunity for quick, guided practice.

The ten Warm Ups feature short reading passages that include examples of the genres that students are required to read and will encounter on the test. In grade 4, the Common Core State Standards require students to read stories, drama, poetry, social studies, science, and technical texts.

Fairy Tale

Poetry

Science Text

Technical/How-to

The questions that follow the Warm Ups include the variety of formats and question types that students will encounter on the new assessments. They include two-part questions, constructed response (short answer) questions, and questions that replicate the technology-enhanced items.

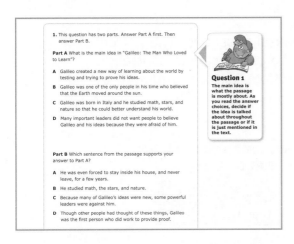

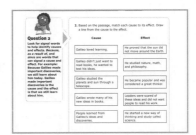

The Warm Ups also include prompts with each question. These prompts provide students with tips and strategies for answering the questions.

Question 2
You can usually find the causes and effects of events in the same paragraph. Skim the passage and find each event. Then read the sentences around it to find out the effects.

Question 1
Authors use details to support an idea. Read each statement and ask yourself if it supports the idea that the Impressionists changed the way people painted.

Question 3
Reread the beginning of the story, paying close attention to the conversation between Angela and her mother. How does Angela's mother show that she knows Angela is having a hard time adjusting?

Practice Tests to Build Test-Taking Stamina

The Practice Tests feature longer passages that match the passage lengths that will be used for the PARCC and Smarter Balanced tests. These passages provide students with experience reading the longer and more complex texts they will have to read on the new assessments.

Two of the Practice Tests also feature paired passages. The paired passages give students the opportunity to compare and contrast texts and integrate information from multiple texts, as required by Standard R.9.

Literature

Informational Text

Paired Texts

Each passage is followed by a complete set of questions that reflects the number of questions students will find with each passage on the new assessments. In addition, similar to the Warm Ups, the Practice Tests also include the types of questions students will encounter. Every Practice Test also includes three constructed response (short answer) questions to give students practice writing about texts and using details from the text in their response.

1. This question has two parts. Answer Part A first. Then answer Part B.

Part A What did the bud want most of all at the beginning of the poem?

A to grow bigger than any other

B to drink the dew that fell on her

C to be more beautiful than her sisters

D to have stars shine and twinkle on her

Part B Which line from the poem supports the answer to Part A?

A And I should be fairer than all my sister flowers.

B Just then a tiny dew-drop that hung o'er the dell

C I would be fair and stately, with a bright star to shine

D But a star would glitter brightly through the long summer hours

Two-part questions

4. Check the boxes of the lessons that can be learned from the poem, "The Flower's Lesson."

☐ Be happy with who you are.

☐ Live and let live.

☐ Might makes right.

☐ Do not try to be something you are not.

☐ One good turn deserves another.

☐ Think before you act.

☐ There are two sides to every truth.

Questions with multiple answers

8. How does the reader know that the mother rose cares deeply for her bud? Use examples from the poem to support your answer.

_____

_____

_____

_____

_____

_____

_____

9. Describe the way in which the bud got hurt. Use details from the poem to support your answer.

_____

_____

_____

_____

_____

_____

10. Retell the poem's story of the bud in three or four sentences. Use key details from the story in your retelling.

_____

_____

_____

_____

_____

_____

_____

_____

_____

_____

_____

_____

Constructed-response questions

Correlated to the Common Core State Standards

All of the assessment items are correlated to the Reading Standards for Literature or the Reading Standards for Informational Text. The correlation chart below shows the standards that each Warm Up and Practice Test addresses.

TEST	RL/RI 4.1	RL/RI 4.2	RL/RI 4.3	RL/RI 4.4	RL/RI 4.5	RL/RI 4.6	RL/RI 4.7	RL/RI 4.8	RL/RI 4.9
Warm Up 1	X		X	X					
Warm Up 2	X			X				X	
Warm Up 3		X		X	X				
Warm Up 4		X	X	X					
Warm Up 5	X		X		X				
Warm Up 6	X	X	X				X		
Warm Up 7	X	X	X						
Warm Up 8	X	X			X			X	
Warm Up 9	X	X	X						
Warm Up 10	X			X			X		
Practice Test 1	X	X	X	X					
Practice Test 2	X	X	X	X	X			X	
Practice Test 3	X	X	X	X	X				X
Practice Test 4	X	X	X	X				X	X

Grade 4 Common Core State Standards

Reading Standards for Literature

RL.4.1 Refer to details and examples in a text when explaining what the text says explicitly and when drawing inferences from the text.

RL.4.2 Determine a theme of a story, drama, or poem from details in the text; summarize the text.

RL.4.3 Describe in depth a character, setting, or event in a story or drama, drawing on specific details in the text (e.g., a character's thoughts, words, or actions).

RL.4.4 Determine the meaning of words and phrases as they are used in a text, including those that allude to significant characters found in mythology (e.g., *Herculean*).

RL.4.5 Explain major differences between poems, drama, and prose, and refer to the structural elements of poems (e.g., verse, rhythm, meter) and drama (e.g., casts of characters, settings, descriptions, dialogue, stage directions) when writing or speaking about a text.

RL.4.6 Compare and contrast the point of view from which different stories are narrated, including the difference between first- and third-person narrations.

RL.4.7 Make connections between the text of a story or drama and a visual or oral presentation of the text, identifying where each version reflects specific descriptions and directions in the text.

RL.4.9 Compare and contrast the treatment of similar themes and topics (e.g., opposition of good and evil) and patterns of events (e.g., the quest) in stories, myths, and traditional literature from different cultures.

Reading Standards for Informational Texts

RI.4.1 Refer to details and examples in a text when explaining what the text says explicitly and when drawing inferences from the text.

RI.4.2 Determine the main idea of a text and explain how it is supported by key details; summarize the text.

RI.4.3 Explain events, procedures, ideas, or concepts in a historical, scientific, or technical text, including what happened and why, based on specific information in the text.

RI.4.4 Determine the meaning of general academic and domain-specific words or phrases in a text relevant to a *grade 4 topic or subject area*.

RI.4.5 Describe the overall structure (e.g., chronology, comparison, cause/effect, problem/solution) of events, ideas, concepts, or information in a text or part of a text.

RI.4.6 Compare and contrast a firsthand and secondhand account of the same event or topic; describe the differences in focus and the information provided.

RI.4.7 Interpret information presented visually, orally, or quantitatively (e.g., in charts, graphs, diagrams, time lines, animations, or interactive elements on Web pages) and explain how the information contributes to an understanding of the text in which it appears.

RI.4.8 Explain how an author uses reasons and evidence to support particular points in a text.

RI.4.9 Integrate information from two texts on the same topic in order to write or speak about the subject knowledgeably.

How to Use Common Core Reading Warm Ups and Practice Tests

The Warm Ups are designed to be quick and easy practice for students. They can be used in a variety of ways:

- Assign Warm Ups for homework.

- Use them for quick review in class.

- Use them for targeted review of key standards. The correlation chart on page 10 can help identify Warm Ups that address the skills you want to focus on.

The longer Practice Tests can be used to prepare students in the weeks before the assessments. They can also be used to help assess students' reading comprehension throughout the year.

Tear-out Answer Keys

Find the answers to all the Warm Ups and Practice Tests in the Answer Key. The Answer Key includes the standards correlations for each question. In addition, it includes sample answers for the constructed response (short answer) questions.

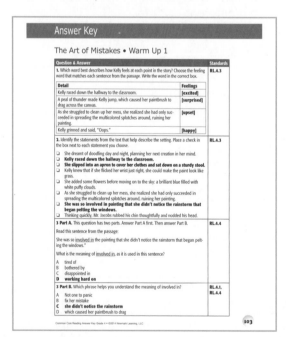

©ommon ©ore ELA STANDARDS

RL.4.1
Refer to details and examples in a text when explaining what the text says explicitly and when drawing inferences from the text.

RL.4.3
Describe in depth a character, setting, or event in a story or drama, drawing on specific details in the text (e.g., a character's thoughts, words, or actions).

RL.4.4
Determine the meaning of words and phrases as they are used in a text, including those that allude to significant characters found in mythology (e.g., *Herculean*).

Read this passage and then answer the questions that follow.

The Art of Mistakes

1   Kelly raced down the hallway to the classroom. It was her favorite part of the day: art class. She dreamt of doodling day and night, planning her next creation in her mind. Would she do a charcoal sketch today or try a watercolor landscape? The possibilities were as endless as the tools at her fingertips: the paintbrushes and pencils, the crayons and colors.

2   She slipped into an apron to cover her clothes and sat down on a sturdy stool. Like a master chess player, she looked at the blank canvas before her, considering where to begin. Then, dipping her thin brush into a dab of green paint, she began to cover the white background with long, even strokes. Kelly knew that if she flicked her wrist just right, she could make the paint look like grass. She added some flowers before moving on to the sky: a brilliant blue filled with white puffy clouds.

continued ➡

3   *It's missing something*, Kelly thought. *A tree—the perfect finishing touch!*

4   She was so involved in painting that she didn't notice the rainstorm that began pelting the windows. A peal of thunder made Kelly jump, which caused her paintbrush to drag across the canvas. Not one to panic, Kelly reached over to grab a rag to fix her mistake, but she spilled a jar of paint in the process. As she struggled to clean up her mess, she realized she had only succeeded in spreading the multicolored splotches around, ruining her painting.

5   Mr. Jacobs, the art teacher, saw that Kelly was upset, and one look at her painting explained everything. Thinking quickly, Mr. Jacobs rubbed his chin thoughtfully and nodded his head.

6   "I see you're trying to experiment with some new techniques. What is this painting called?"

7   Kelly grinned and said, "Oops."

Name_____ Date_____

1. Which word best describes how Kelly feels at each point in the story? Choose the feeling word that matches each sentence from the passage. Write the word in the correct box.

surprised	excited	embarrassed	angry
sorry	upset	happy	

Detail	Feelings
Kelly raced down the hallway to the classroom.	
A peal of thunder made Kelly jump, which caused her paintbrush to drag across the canvas.	
As she struggled to clean up her mess, she realized she had only succeeded in spreading the multicolored splotches around, ruining her painting.	
Kelly grinned and said, "Oops."	

Question 1

To answer this question, you will need to look for clues in the text and then make inferences about the character. The sentence "Kelly raced down the hall" could show that Kelly was in a rush or running away. But because the text also says that art was Kelly's favorite part of the day, the reader can infer that Kelly is excited.

continued

Name_____ Date_____

Question 2

The setting is where and when a story takes place. Where does "The Art of Mistakes" take place? Which of the statements help you picture Kelly's surroundings?

2. Identify the statements from the text that help describe the setting. Place a check in the box next to each statement you choose.

☐ She dreamt of doodling day and night, planning her next creation in her mind.

☐ Kelly raced down the hallway to the classroom.

☐ She slipped into an apron to cover her clothes and sat down on a sturdy stool.

☐ She added some flowers before moving on to the sky: a brilliant blue filled with white puffy clouds.

☐ As she struggled to clean up her mess, she realized she had only succeeded in spreading the multicolored splotches around, ruining her painting.

☐ She was so involved in painting that she didn't notice the rainstorm that began pelting the windows.

☐ Thinking quickly, Mr. Jacobs rubbed his chin thoughtfully and nodded his head.

Name_____ Date_____

3. This question has two parts. Answer Part A first. Then answer Part B.

Part A Read this sentence from the passage:

> She was so <u>involved in</u> the painting that she didn't notice the rainstorm that began pelting the windows.

What is the meaning of <u>involved in</u>, as it is used in this sentence?

A tired of

B bothered by

C disappointed in

D working hard on

Question 3

Replace *involved in* with each answer choice. If the meaning of the sentence changes, you can eliminate it as an answer choice.

Part B Which phrase helps you understand the meaning of <u>involved in</u>?

A Not one to panic

B fix her mistake

C she didn't notice the rainstorm

D which caused her paintbrush to drag

STOP!

RI.4.1
Refer to details and examples in a text when explaining what the text says explicitly and when drawing inferences from the text.

RI.4.4
Determine the meaning of general academic and domain-specific words or phrases in a text relevant to a grade 4 topic or subject area.

RI.4.8
Explain how an author uses reasons and evidence to support particular points in a text.

Read this passage and then answer the questions that follow.

The Start of Something New

1   In nineteenth-century France, there was only one "acceptable" style of painting. This art sought to look realistic and the subjects were always religious or historic. At art shows, the paintings were all very similar. How is it that today's art museums feature so many different styles? Many say it all began with a group of men and women called the Impressionists.

2   It was 1874 in Paris; a group of artists were attempting something new. Unlike the other artists of their time, these painters used surprising colors; vague, blurry shapes; and hurried-looking brushstrokes to represent the objects they painted. Art experts were astonished at this new approach. "It looks like a mere *impression*," someone said, criticizing a now-famous painting. This insult effectively named the movement. Impressionism had begun, with or without the art world's approval.

3   Some Impressionists, like Pierre-Auguste Renoir and Claude Monet, spent years studying one subject alone, like dancers or water lilies. They painted the same things repeatedly, in different lights and colors, highlighting motion and feeling. Other painters chose subjects like parks or sailboats. The Impressionists' breathtaking artwork taught critics that there were more things worth painting than royalty and religion. Exploring the beauty in smaller things, these artists captured the vibrancy of life as no one had before.

4   Many Impressionists lived in poverty because their paintings did not sell well. People were slow to like the artwork because it was so different. But the Impressionists did not change. They knew their work was beautiful and important—and today, their costly paintings hang in the world's greatest museums, proving that they were right.

5   Impressionism opened doors for other artists to try new creative styles. Today, there is no "correct" way of painting. The Impressionists taught us that there is always room for fresh ways to see color and life.

continued ▶

Name_____ Date_____

Question 1

Authors use details to support an idea. Read each statement and ask yourself if it supports the idea that the Impressionists changed the way people painted.

1. Read this sentence from the passage.

> How is it that today's art museums feature so many different styles? Many say it all began with a group of men and women called the Impressionists.

Select the details the author uses to support this idea. Check the box next to each statement you choose.

❑ This insult effectively named the movement.

❑ Impressionism opened the doors for other artists to try new creative styles.

❑ The Impressionists' breathtaking artwork taught critics that there were more things worth painting than royalty and religion.

❑ Some Impressionists, like Pierre-Auguste Renoir and Claude Monet, spent years studying one subject alone, like dancers or water lilies.

❑ Unlike the other artists of their time, these painters used surprising colors; vague, blurry shapes; and hurried-looking brushstrokes to represent the objects they painted.

❑ They painted the same things repeatedly, in different lights and colors, highlighting motion and feeling.

❑ Today, there is no "correct" way of painting.

❑ Many Impressionists lived in poverty because their paintings did not sell well.

Name_____ Date_____

2. Which detail from the text supports the inference that today people admire and value the work of the Impressionists?

A   They knew their work was beautiful and important.

B   These artists captured the vibrancy of life as no one had before.

C   Today, their costly paintings hang in the world's greatest museums.

D   People were slow to like the artwork.

Question 2

The main idea is what the text is mostly about. If a statement contains a minor detail, you can eliminate it as an answer choice. In this passage, a minor detail would have been the title of one of the paintings or the year that one of the artists was born.

3. Read this sentence from the passage:

> This art sought to look realistic and the subjects were always <u>religious</u> or historic.

What is the meaning of <u>religious</u> as it is used in this sentence?

A   like a photograph

B   having to do with God

C   about the royal family

D   important to French people

Question 3

Identifying the root word of an unfamiliar word can help you identify the meaning. In this case, the root word of *religious* is *religion*.

STOP!

common ore ELA
STANDARDS

RL.4.2
Determine a theme of a story, drama, or poem from details in the text; summarize the text.

RL.4.4
Determine the meaning of words and phrases as they are used in a text, including those that allude to significant characters found in mythology (e.g., *Herculean*).

RL.4.5
Explain major differences between poems, drama, and prose, and refer to the structural elements of poems (e.g., verse, rhythm, meter) and drama (e.g., casts of characters, settings, descriptions, dialogue, stage directions) when writing or speaking about a text.

Read this passage and then answer the questions that follow.

Don't Give Up

by Phoebe Cary

If you've tried and have not won,
Never stop for crying;
All's that's great and good is done
Just by patient trying.

5   Though young birds, in flying, fall,
Still their wings grow stronger;
And the next time they can keep
Up a little longer.

Though the sturdy oak has known
10   Many a blast that bowed her,
She has risen again, and grown
Loftier and prouder.

If by easy work you beat,
Who the more will prize you?
15   Gaining victory from defeat,—
That's the test that tries you!

Name_____ Date_____

1. What is the theme of the poem?

A winning

B keep trying

C learning to fly

D not taking risks

Question 1

In some poems, the theme is stated at the beginning or end of a text, or both. Reread the first and last stanzas of the poem and look for clues about the theme.

2. What does the phrase <u>gaining victory from defeat</u> mean in this poem?

A to earn a prize

B to fail an easy test

C to succeed after failing

D to win against a losing team

Question 2

To understand the meaning of a phrase, think about what each word means by itself. Ask yourself the meanings of *gaining*, *victory*, and *defeat*. Then think about what they mean together in the phrase.

continued

Name_____ Date_____

Question 3

Remember that a stanza is a grouping of lines in a poem. Poets use stanzas to organize a poem in the same way that writers use paragraphs in prose. To answer this question, reread one stanza at a time and then read the details one at a time. Ask yourself if each detail applies to the stanza. Repeat this with all four stanzas.

3. Match each detail listed below with the correct stanza in the poem. Write the stanza number (1, 2, 3, or 4) in the box next to each detail. If a detail applies to more than one stanza, write each correct number in the box.

Details	Stanza
Lines one and three rhyme.	
Birds get stronger each time they try to fly.	
You should not waste time feeling sorry for yourself.	
Lines two and four rhyme.	
It is best to succeed doing something difficult.	
The oak tree grew taller after winds bowed it.	
Great things happen when people don't give up.	

Common Core ELA STANDARDS

RI.4.2
Determine the main idea of a text and explain how it is supported by key details; summarize the text.

RI.4.3
Explain events, procedures, ideas, or concepts in a historical, scientific, or technical text, including what happened and why, based on specific information in the text.

RI.4.4
Determine the meaning of general academic and domain-specific words or phrases in a text relevant to a grade 4 topic or subject area.

Read this passage and then answer the questions that follow.

Swimming

from the CDC's Swimming Activity Card
http://www.cdc.gov/bam/activity/cards/swimming.html

1   Swimming is more than a great way to cool off when it's hot; it's also a fun activity that helps you work out your whole body. If you don't know how to swim, or if you want to brush up your skills, you'll want to take some lessons at your local pool. There, you'll master the basics to help keep your head above water.

2   There are some basic moves that beginners learn when they first hit the water. Beginners learn to float and they learn to tread water. Both of the skills help beginners feel more comfortable in the water.

continued ➤

Floating

3   Our bodies have a natural tendency[1] to float—so go with it! Relax and let the water support your body. Lie back with your arms stretched out to the side. Turn your palms up and keep the backs of your hands in the water. Arch your back, stretch out your legs (some gentle kicking will help you float more easily), and take short breaths to stay relaxed. Floating is a great way to relax, or to rest while you call for help if you don't have enough energy to swim to shore or to the side of a pool.

Treading Water

4   Another way to keep afloat is to tread water. Get into the water and pretend you are gently riding a bicycle, with your back straight and your arms straight out in front of you. While you're moving your legs, sweep your arms together with your palms facing down and in. Then, sweep them back out with your palms facing down and away from each other.

5   Now that you know how to keep your head above the water, try swimming with your head below water!

[1]Incline towards.

Name_____ Date_____

1. This question has two parts. Answer Part A first. Then answer Part B.

Part A What is the main idea of "Swimming"?

A the correct way to move your arms in water

B ways to keep your head above water

C where to sign up for swimming lessons

D how to get help in a swimming emergency

Part B Which detail from the text supports the answer to Part A?

A Swimming is more than a great way to cool off when it's hot.

B While you're moving your legs, sweep your arms together with your palms facing down and in.

C Another way to keep afloat is to tread water.

D If you don't know how to swim, or if you want to brush up your skills, you'll want to take some lessons at your local pool.

Question 1

In nonfiction texts, the main idea is often identified in the introduction. It may also be mentioned again in the conclusion. Reread the introduction and conclusion and look for the main idea.

continued

Name_____ Date_____

Question 2

Some words have multiple meanings. It's important to look at how the word is used in the text. In this case, the passage says "brush up your skills" and "take some lessons." These are both clues to the meaning of the phrase *brush up*.

2. What is the meaning of the phrase <u>brush up</u> in paragraph 1?

A to scrub or polish

B to practice

C to clean

D to learn

3. Read each description and decide whether it applies to floating or treading water. Write the letter in the correct column.

Floating	Treading Water

Question 3

Reread the paragraph on floating. As you read each step of how to float, look for it in the list of answer choices. If you find it in the list, place a check by it and write the letter in the appropriate column.

A arch your back

B let the water support your body

C pretend you are riding a bicycle

D kick your legs gently

E keep your back straight

F stretch your arms out to the side

G sweep your arms together and back out

H take short breaths

STOP!

Common Core ELA STANDARDS

RL.4.1
Refer to details and examples in a text when explaining what the text says explicitly and when drawing inferences from the text.

RL.4.3
Describe in depth a character, setting, or event in a story or drama, drawing on specific details in the text (e.g., a character's thoughts, words, or actions).

RL.4.5
Explain major differences between poems, drama, and prose, and refer to the structural elements of poems (e.g., verse, rhythm, meter) and drama (e.g., casts of characters, settings, descriptions, dialogue, stage directions) when writing or speaking about a text.

Read this passage and then answer the questions that follow.

from "Gareth and Lynette"

An excerpt from *Stories of King Arthur's Knights told to the*

***Children* by Mary MacGregor**

1 Gareth was a little prince. His home was an old gray castle, and there were great mountains all round the castle. Gareth loved these mountains and his beautiful home at the foot of them. He had lived there all his life.

2 Gareth had no little boys or girls to play with, for there were no houses near his mountain home.

3 But Gareth was happy all day long. Sometimes in the bright summer mornings the streams would call to him. Then he would follow them up the mountains, till he found the place where the streams ended in tiny silver threads.

continued ▶

4   Sometimes the birds and beasts, his woodland friends, would call to him, and then Gareth would wander about in the forest with them till evening came. Then he would tell his mother the wonderful things he had seen, and the wonderful things he had heard in the forests and on the mountain-sides.

5   Gareth's mother, the Queen of Orkney, loved the little prince so much that she was never dull. She had no one to talk to except her little son, for her husband was old, so old that he could not talk to his Queen. And if she talked to him, he was almost too deaf to hear what she said.

6   But though the Queen was never dull, she was sometimes unhappy. She was afraid that some day, when Gareth was older, he would want to leave her to go into the world, perhaps to go to the great King Arthur's court, as his three brothers had done.

7   Now Gareth had already heard stories about the brave deeds of King Arthur's knights. He knew that they were strong men, and that they fought for the weak people, and that they often had great adventures, when they were sent to punish the King's enemies. And Gareth longed to be a man, for "when I am a man, I will be one of Arthur's knights, too," he thought.

Name_____ Date_____

1. This question has two parts. Answer Part A first. Then answer Part B.

Part A What inference can you make from the passage?

A   The queen worried that Gareth would get hurt while playing in the forest.

B   The queen did not love her other sons as much as she loved Gareth.

C   Gareth wanted to join King Arthur's court to be with his brothers.

D   Gareth told his mother about his adventures because he had no friends and his father could not hear well and did not speak.

Question 1

An inference is a logical guess a reader makes based on details in a text. Read the passage again and underline the details that support each answer choice. If you cannot find details, you can eliminate that answer choice.

Part B Which detail from the story supports the answer to Part A?

A   She was afraid that some day, when Gareth was older, he would want to leave her to go into the world, perhaps to go to the great King Arthur's court, as his three brothers had done.

B   Gareth had no little boys or girls to play with, for there were no houses near his mountain home.

C   Sometimes the birds and beasts, his woodland friends, would call to him, and then Gareth would wander about in the forest with them till evening came.

D   Then he would follow them up the mountains, till he found the place where the streams ended in tiny silver threads.

continued

Name_____ Date_____

Question 2

Think about how a play is different from a story. Stories are often divided into chapters. How are plays divided? How do plays tell the reader what action is taking place?

Question 3

Reread the story and underline any details about the characters. Then look at the descriptions listed in the questions. Do any of the details you identified support a description. For example, paragraph 4 describes Gareth wandering in the forests all day. Which description does that support? If you find it, determine which person it applies to and write the letter under that character's name. If you do not find it, cross it off the list.

2. If this story were turned into a play, which new elements would be added?

☐ character development

☐ dialogue

☐ a cast of characters

☐ stage directions

☐ stanzas

☐ acts or scenes

☐ a setting

3. Which of the descriptions below best fit the character Gareth and which best fit the queen? Choose four descriptions for each character and write the letters below the character's name.

Gareth	The Queen

A adventurous

B never bored

C unhappy

D cheerful

E entertaining

F worried

G loves nature

H does not want to be alone

STOP!

Common Core ELA STANDARDS

RI.4.1
Refer to details and examples in a text when explaining what the text says explicitly and when drawing inferences from the text.

RI.4.2
Determine the main idea of a text and explain how it is supported by key details; summarize the text.

RI.4.3
Explain events, procedures, ideas, or concepts in a historical, scientific, or technical text, including what happened and why, based on specific information in the text.

RI.4.7
Interpret information presented visually, orally, or quantitatively (e.g., in charts, graphs, diagrams, time lines, animations, or interactive elements on Web pages) and explain how the information contributes to an understanding of the text in which it appears.

Read this passage and then answer the questions that follow.

Special Quarters

1   The U.S. quarter dollar (commonly known as "the quarter") has been produced since 1796. The silver coins were first minted with a profile of Lady Liberty on the front and a small bald eagle on the back.

2   Then, in 1932, the Washington Quarter was released. It was designed by John Flanagan as a special commemorative coin. It became a regular-issue coin in 1934.

3   The next change to the design of the quarter came in 1999. That's when the 50 State Quarters program began. The program was created to encourage a new generation of coin collectors.

4   With the program, the U.S. Mint released a new quarter every ten weeks, or five new quarters each year. The quarters contained Washington's likeness on the front and a unique state design on the reverse side. The coins were released in the same order the states joined the union, starting with Delaware and ending with Hawaii.

continued →

5   The 50 State Quarters program was the most popular commemorative coin program in our country's history. For 33 states, the governors chose the final designs. For 17 of the quarters, 3.5 million Americans voted on the state images. About half of the U.S. population collected the coins. The U.S. government made a profit of more than $3 billion from people who collected the coins, taking them out of circulation.

6   In 2010, a new program, America the Beautiful Quarters, began. In 2021, when the program ends, 56 new quarters will have been released. Each quarter will feature a different national site from each state and territory in the United States. The first coin released featured Hot Springs National Park in Arkansas, while the final coin will honor the Tuskegee Airmen National Historic Site in Alabama. Happy collecting!

America the Beautiful Quarter Designs* 2010–2012

Year	Reverse Design	State
2010	Hot Springs National Park	Arkansas
	Yellowstone National Park	Wyoming
	Yosemite National Park	California
	Grand Canyon National Park	Arizona
	Mt. Hood National Forest	Oregon
2011	Gettysburg National Military Park	Pennsylvania
	Glacier National Park	Montana
	Olympic National Park	Washington
	Vicksburg National Military Park	Mississippi
	Chickasaw National Recreational Area	Oklahoma
2012	El Yunque National Forest	Puerto Rico
	Chaco Culture National Historical Park	New Mexico
	Acadia National Park	Maine
	Hawaii Volcanoes National Park	Hawaii
	Denali National Park Preserve	Alaska

*All quarters feature the 1932 portrait of George Washington by John Flanagan on the front.

Common Core Reading Warm-Ups & Test Practice Grade 4 • ©2014 Newmark Learning, LLC

Name_____ Date_____

1. This question has two parts. Answer Part A first. Then answer Part B.

Part A What is the main idea of the passage?

A   why the quarter was created

B   how to start a quarter collection

C   why Washington is on the quarter

D   how quarters have changed over time

Part B Which detail from the passage supports the answer to Part A?

A   The next change to the design of the quarter came in 1999.

B   The program was created to encourage a new generation of coin collectors.

C   The U.S. quarter dollar (commonly known as "the quarter") has been produced since 1796.

D   The U.S. government made a profit of more than $3 billion from people who collected the coins, taking them out of circulation.

Question 1

The *main idea* is what the passage is mostly about. Read paragraphs 2, 3, and 4 again. What do these paragraphs have in common? Use this information to help you determine the main idea.

continued

Name_____ Date_____

Question 2

You can usually find the causes and effects of events in the same paragraph. Skim the passage and find each event. Then read the sentences around it to find out the effects.

2. Based on the passage, choose the cause of each effect listed. Draw a line connecting each cause to its effect.

Cause	Effect
Half of Americans collected the 50 State Quarters.	Fifty-six new quarters will have been released by 2021.
The 50 State Quarters program was created.	The U.S. government made more than $3 billion.
The America the Beautiful Quarters program was created.	New people became interested in coin collecting.

Name_____ Date_____

3. Use the text and the chart to determine which statements are correct. Check the box next to each statement you choose.

☐ The America the Beautiful Quarters program is to run from 2010 until 2021.

☐ Five quarters will be released each year.

☐ Grand Canyon National Park was featured in 2011.

☐ The front of each quarter will have a portrait of George Washington.

☐ U.S. territories will not be included in the America the Beautiful Quarters program.

☐ A total of 56 America the Beautiful Quarters will be released.

☐ The America the Beautiful Quarters from Alabama is already available.

☐ Mt. Hood National Forest is in Puerto Rico.

☐ The first design in 2011 featured Gettysburg National Military Park.

☐ Acadia National Park is in Maine.

Question 3

This question asks you to find information in both the passage and the chart. First, reread the paragraph in the passage that describes the America the Beautiful Quarters program. As you read a fact in the paragraph, look for it in the answer choices and check it off. Next, reread the chart and look for each unchecked answer choice. If you find the information in the chart, check it off.

continued ➡

Name_____ Date_____

Question 4

To answer this question, you will need to make an inference, or a logical guess, and then find details to support your answer. In this passage, the reader can infer that the U.S. Mint started a new program because first program was so successful. Underline any details in the text that support that inference and use them in your answer.

4. Why do you think the U.S. Mint started the America the Beautiful Quarters program? Use details from the text to support your answer.

_____

_____

_____

_____

_____

_____

⊙ommon ⊙ore ELA STANDARDS

RL.4.1
Refer to details and examples in a text when explaining what the text says explicitly and when drawing inferences from the text.

RL.4.2
Determine a theme of a story, drama, or poem from details in the text; summarize the text.

RL.4.3
Describe in depth a character, setting, or event in a story or drama, drawing on specific details in the text (e.g., a character's thoughts, words, or actions).

Read this passage and then answer the questions that follow.

A Golden Riddle

1   Long ago, in a faraway kingdom, there lived a brave knight. He was the queen's favorite, so when a chest of gold went missing, she ordered him to the throne room and demanded, "Find that chest, my fearless knight!"

2   Atop a high mountain, in a dark cave, the knight discovered the chest, a huge dragon curled around it. The knight stood boldly before the fearsome beast as it announced, "I know why you have come to my lair—you want to steal my chest of gold!"

3   "That chest of gold belongs to the queen, not to you," the knight retorted.

4   "Finders keepers," rumbled the dragon. "But I am willing to make you a deal: I will give you back the gold if you can solve my riddle; but if you cannot, I get to keep the chest of gold."

5   "Speak your riddle then."

continued ➡

6 The dragon smiled, showing all of his sharp teeth, and said, "What creature loves gold more than I do, but always leaves it behind?"

7 The knight was stumped; everyone knows that dragons love gold more than any person or any thing. He could not come up with an answer.

8 The dragon taunted, "Do you give up?"

9 "Not yet! Give me a minute to think." The knight paced, trying to puzzle it out. He wandered over to the mouth of the cave and looked down at the castle far below. He was afraid he would fail the queen. The knight pictured her in the royal garden, surrounded by all of her yellow sunflowers.

10 "I know the answer!" exclaimed the knight. "The gold you speak of is the pollen of the sunflowers, and the creature that loves that gold more than you is the bee."

11 The dragon growled, fire escaping from his mouth. "Take the chest, Knight. You have won."

Name_____ Date_____

1. This question has two parts. Answer Part A first. Then answer Part B.

Part A Which statement is a theme of "A Golden Riddle"?

A Fear can make people fail.

B Taking risks is often dangerous.

C Wealth makes people powerful.

D Knowledge is more important than strength.

Question 1

To identify a theme, look for an idea that is talked about at least two times in the story. For example, in this story the knight does take a dangerous risk looking for the gold. But there are not many details about the danger the knight is facing.

Part B Which detail from the text supports the answer to Part A?

A The knight was stumped; everyone knows that dragons love gold more than any person or any thing.

B The dragon growled, fire escaping from his mouth.

C "I will give you back the gold if you can solve my riddle; but if you cannot, I get to keep the chest of gold."

D "Finders keepers," rumbled the dragon.

continued

Name_____ Date_____

Question 2

An inference is made from clues the author gives readers. Look for clues to support each statement. If you cannot find clues to support a statement, you can eliminate it as an answer choice.

Question 3

To answer this question, first trying matching each character trait with an action. Which of the actions would fit a character who is clever? Which action shows that a character is fierce or tough? Jot the letter of the action next to the letter of the trait. Then match each character with an action.

2. Which of the following can you infer from the text?

A   The knight is loyal to his queen.

B   The queen is afraid of dragons.

C   The cave is not far from the castle.

D   The dragon will steal the gold back.

3. Choose a trait to describe each character in the story. Write the letter next to the character's name in the Trait column. Then choose an action that reveals that trait. Write the letter next to the character's name in the Action column.

Character	Trait	Action
Dragon		
Knight		
Queen		

Trait:

A commanding

B fearful

C fierce

D clever

Action:

E solved a riddle

F showed sharp teeth

G gave an order

H paced the floor

Name_____ Date_____

4. Summarize "A Golden Riddle" in your own words.

_____

_____

_____

_____

_____

_____

_____

_____

_____

Question 4

A summary should include only the most important events in a story. One way to start a summary is to jot down what the problem was in the story and what the solution was.

RI.4.1
Refer to details and examples in a text when explaining what the text says explicitly and when drawing inferences from the text.

RI.4.2
Determine the main idea of a text and explain how it is supported by key details; summarize the text.

RI.4.5
Describe the overall structure (e.g., chronology, comparison, cause/effect, problem/solution) of events, ideas, concepts, or information in a text or part of a text.

RI.4.8
Explain how an author uses reasons and evidence to support particular points in a text.

Read this passage and then answer the questions that follow.

Our Friend the Bat

1   Bats are among the world's most interesting and amazing creatures. There are more than 1,000 different species of bats in the world. These range from large bats that measure almost 6 feet from wing to wing, to tiny bats that are no bigger than your finger.

2   Bats can live alone or in groups. A group of bats living together is called a colony. Bats have many different habitats; they can live in decaying trees, in caves, and even under bridges. Some people put up special houses for bats.

3   The diet of a bat is varied, ranging from insects to fruit to small animals such as mice and birds. Most of the bats that live in the United States and Canada eat insects, like beetles, flies, and gnats. In fact, a single bat can eat 2,000 to 6,000 insects in one night!

4   Many people are frightened of bats, but unnecessarily so. They believe that bats will attack humans and get stuck in their hair. However, bats are not vicious, and they rarely bother people.

5   Bats can actually help us in many ways. For instance, they aid farmers by eating insects that destroy crops. Bats also keep mosquito populations down. Bats are pollinators, too; they carry pollen from one plant to another to help plants disperse their seeds and reproduce. In rain forests, bats help new plant life begin by spreading the seeds of plants or trees that have been cut down and burned. This helps plant life continue to flourish.

6   Today many people recognize that bats are an important part of a healthy environment and that it is crucial to keep these winged mammals protected and safe.

continued

Name_____ Date_____

1. This question has two parts. Answer Part A first. Then answer Part B.

Part A What is the main idea of "Our Friend the Bat"?

A Bats make excellent pets.

B Bats are interesting animals.

C Bats eat many different things.

D Bats are dangerous to humans.

Part B Which detail from the passage supports the answer to Part A?

A Some people put up special houses for bats.

B Many people are frightened of bats, but unnecessarily so.

C Bats are among the world's most interesting and amazing creatures.

D The diet of a bat is varied, ranging from insects to fruit to small animals such as mice and birds.

Question 1

In informational texts, the main idea is sometimes stated in the introduction. Reread the introduction and underline what you think is the main idea. Read the answer choices in Part B. Do any of these details support the main idea you have identified?

Name_____ Date_____

Question 2

To identify how the author has organized the information in this passage, underline a phrase or sentence in each paragraph that states the main idea of the paragraph.

2. How is the information in this passage organized?

A Each paragraph focuses on a different type of bat.

B Each paragraph explains a different myth about bats.

C Each paragraph discusses a different topic related to bats.

D Each paragraph describes a different way bats are helpful.

3. Which of the following inferences can you make from the passage "Our Friend the Bat"? Place a checkmark in the box next to each statement you choose.

❏ Bats carry germs.

❏ The author is scared of bats.

❏ The author thinks bats have been unfairly judged.

❏ Earth needs bats.

❏ Bats keep our water clean.

❏ The author likes bats.

❏ Some people keep bats as pets.

❏ Bats compete with humans for food.

Question 3

An inference has to be based on evidence in the text. For example, it may be true that some people keep bats as pets. But does the author provide any information about this topic in the passage? If not, "Some people keep bats as pets" is not a correct choice for question 3.

continued ➤

Name_____ Date_____

4. What is the author's point of view on the role of bats in the environment? What two details does the author use to support this point of view?

_____

_____

_____

_____

_____

_____

Question 4

In paragraph 6, the author states that bats are a part of a healthy environment. Reread the passage and underline any details that support this idea. Then use the details as part of your answer.

common ore ELA STANDARDS

RL.4.1
Refer to details and examples in a text when explaining what the text says explicitly and when drawing inferences from the text.

RL.4.2
Determine a theme of a story, drama, or poem from details in the text; summarize the text.

RL.4.3
Describe in depth a character, setting, or event in a story or drama, drawing on specific details in the text (e.g., a character's thoughts, words, or actions).

Read this passage and then answer the questions that follow.

Falling into Place

1   Angela Burton sat on the porch tying the laces of her old, scuffed-up black-and-white sneakers. She had left her new red sneakers in her bedroom closet.

2   Angela's mom sat down next to her. "Why are you wearing your old sneakers?"

3   "I misplaced my new ones," Angela said, shrugging. She was embarrassed to admit the truth to her mother. Everybody at Angela's new school seemed to be wearing black-and-white sneakers. The new sneakers could stay in their box for a while.

4   Without pushing for more information, Angela's mother stood up and headed for the car. Angela grabbed her backpack and followed. A few minutes later, they arrived at Keystone Middle School. "It takes time to adjust to a new place," her mother said. "Just be yourself, and everything will fall into place."

continued ➤

5   On the way into school, Angela smiled at some girls from her class. They didn't seem to notice her. She wondered if she would ever adapt to this new school. A wave of loneliness flooded over Angela. She hoped it wouldn't take forever until she got used to the changes in her life.

6   When Angela entered the fifth-grade classroom, she felt invisible. All of her classmates seemed to be talking together in pairs or groups. No one paid any attention to her. Angela sat at her desk, feeling awkward and self-conscious, until she thought of her mother's words, "Just be yourself."

7   Angela pulled a pad of drawing paper and some colored pencils from her backpack. Drawing, her favorite hobby, always seemed to relax her. As Angela began a picture of her cat, her worries melted away. After a few minutes, Mike and Lucy, two of Angela's classmates, came over to watch.

8   "You're a really good artist," Lucy said, studying Angela's picture with admiration.

9   "My mom's an art teacher," Angela explained. "She showed me how."

10   "I wish I could draw like that," Lucy said with a touch of envy.

11   "I could show you a few tricks my mom taught me," Angela said, as Lucy and Mike pulled their chairs up to her desk.

Name_____ Date_____

1. This question has two parts. Answer Part A first. Then answer Part B.

Part A What inference can you make about Angela from the beginning of "Falling into Place"?

A She is a showoff.

B She wants to fit in.

C She makes new friends easily.

D She likes black better than red.

Part B Which sentence from the passage supports the answer to Part A?

A She had left her new red sneakers in her bedroom closet.

B On the way into school, Angela smiled at some girls from her class.

C Everybody at Angela's new school seemed to be wearing black-and-white sneakers.

D "I could show you a few tricks my mom taught me," Angela said, as Lucy and Mike pulled their chairs up to her desk.

Question 1

Reread paragraphs 1 through 3. Look for details that support each answer choice. If you cannot find any details, you can eliminate the answer choice. For example, are there any details that support the idea that Angela is a showoff?

continued

Name_____ Date_____

Question 2

Remember that a summary includes the most important parts of the story and leaves out personal opinions and minor details. First decide what should be included in the summary. Place an X on the line if the statement is an opinion or if it is a minor detail. Then put the statements that are left into the correct order.

2. Choose five sentences that should be included in a summary of "Falling into Place." Number them in the correct order.

____ Mike and Lucy ask Angela about her drawing.

____ Angela put on her black-and-white sneakers.

____ Angela's mom tells her to be herself and everything will work out.

____ Angela offers to help Lucy and Mike learn to draw.

____ Angela should have introduced herself to her classmates.

____ Because she doesn't have anyone to talk to, Angela begins drawing at her desk.

____ Angela is having a hard time because she is going to a new school.

____ Angela's mother sat next to her on the porch.

Question 3

Reread the beginning of the story, paying close attention to the conversation between Angela and her mother. How does Angela's mother show that she knows Angela is having a hard time adjusting?

3. Which details from the text support the inference that Angela's mother understands how Angela feels? Check the box next to each detail you choose.

☐ "Why are you wearing your old sneakers?"

☐ She was embarrassed to admit the truth to her mother.

☐ Without pushing for more information, Angela's mother stood up and headed for the car.

☐ "Just be yourself, and everything will fall into place."

☐ A few minutes later, they arrived at Keystone Middle School.

☐ Angela's mom sat down next to her.

☐ "My mom's an art teacher," Angela explained.

Name_____ Date_____

4. In "Falling into Place," why did Angela start drawing a
picture at her desk, and what happened as a result?

_____

_____

_____

_____

_____

_____

_____

_____

Question 4

This question has two
parts. It asks *why*
something happened
and *what happened*
as a result. Reread
paragraphs 6 and 7
and underline the
details that tell you
why Angela started
drawing. Then reread
paragraph 8 and look
for details that tell
you *what happened*
as a result. Use these
details to write your
response.

Common Core ELA STANDARDS

RI.4.1
Refer to details and examples in a text when explaining what the text says explicitly and when drawing inferences from the text.

RI.4.4
Determine the meaning of general academic and domain-specific words or phrases in a text relevant to a *grade 4 topic or subject area.*

RI.4.7
Interpret information presented visually, orally, or quantitatively (e.g., in charts, graphs, diagrams, time lines, animations, or interactive elements on Web pages) and explain how the information contributes to an understanding of the text in which it appears.

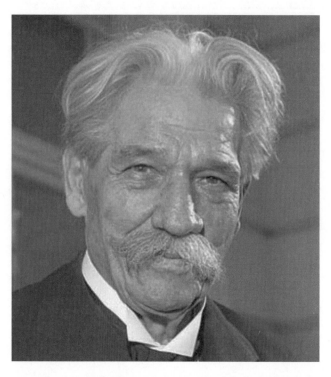

Read this passage and then answer the questions that follow.

Earliest Recollections

from *Memoirs of Childhood and Youth* by Albert Schweitzer

1   One day on the way home from school I had a wrestle with George Nitschelm—he is now underground—who was bigger than me, and was supposed to be stronger, but I got him down. While he was lying under me, he jerked out, "Yes, if I got broth to eat twice a week, as you do, I should be as strong as you are!" I staggered home, overcome by this finish to our play. George Nitschelm had, with cruel plainness, declared what I had already been obliged to feel on other occasions: the village boys did not accept me as one of themselves. I was to them one who was better off than they were, the parson's son, a sprig of the gentry. The certainty of this caused me much suffering, for I wanted to be exactly like them, and not a bit better off. The broth became nauseous to me; whenever I saw it steaming on the table I could hear George Nitschelm's voice.

2   So I now watched most carefully to see that I did not make myself in any way different from the others. For winter wear I had been given an overcoat made out of an old one of my father's. But no village-boy wore an overcoat, and when the tailor was fitting it on and said, "By Jove, Albert, now you're a regular gentleman!" it cost me a big effort to keep back the tears.

3   The day I was to wear it for the first time—it was for church on a Sunday morning—I refused point-blank, and there was an unpleasant scene. They had to take me to church without the overcoat, and every time I was expected to wear it, it was the same tale over again. What a number of times I got the stick over this new garment! But I stood firm.

4   That same winter my mother took me to Strassburg to visit an elderly relative, and she wished to use the visit as an opportunity for buying me a cap. In a fine big shop they tried several on me, and at last my mother and the shopwoman agreed on a handsome sailor's cap which I was to take for my own. But they had reckoned without their host. The cap displeased me altogether, because no village boy wore a sailor's cap. When they went on pressing me to take this one or that one from among all those they had tried on me, I got into such a passion that everybody in the shop ran up to us.

continued →

Name_____ Date_____

5   "Well, what sort of cap *do* you want, you stupid lad?" the
shopwoman shouted at me. "I won't have one of your new-
fashioned ones. I'll have one like what the village boys wear."
So a shop-girl was sent out, and she brought me from the
unsaleable stock a brown cap that one could pull down over
one's ears. Beaming with joy, I put it on while my poor mother
put up with some cutting remarks and some contemptuous
glances on account of her young duffer. It hurt me that she had
been put to shame before the townspeople on my account, but
she did not scold me. It seemed as if she suspected that there
was some real reason behind it all.

6   This stern contest lasted all the time I was at the village
school.

The Life and Work of Albert Schweitzer (1865–1975)

Education	PhD (Doctor of Philosophy) MD (Doctor of Medicine)
Books	Wrote about music, religion, and philosophy
Work	Doctor (physician) university professor organist writer lecturer minister
Major Achievement	Founded hospital in Africa, expanded to 70 buildings; served more than 500 people
Awards	Nobel Peace Prize British Order of Merit French Academy (member)

Name_____ Date_____

Question 1

An inference is a logical guess based on details from the text. Reread the passage and look for details to support each statement. If you cannot find details to support a statement, you cannot make that inference.

1. Which of the following inferences can you make from this passage? Check the box next to each inference you choose.

☐ Albert is not proud of being the parson's son.

☐ The village boys come from poor families.

☐ Albert thinks he is better than the village boys.

☐ Albert's parents want him to dress up for church.

☐ George Nitschelm gets in a lot of fights.

☐ Albert would rather have friends than nice clothes.

☐ Albert does not like going to church.

☐ Mother does not like the village boys.

Question 2

Authors often use figurative language to describe something. In this example, cost does not mean the price of something. Reread the paragraph and look for context clues to help figure out how the author is using the word here.

2. In paragraph 2, what does the author mean when he says "it cost me a big effort to keep back the tears."

A It would take a lot of money for him to cry.

B It was hard for him not to cry.

C It was hard work to cry.

D It was difficult for him to cry.

continued

Name_____ Date_____

3. This question has two parts. Answer Part A first. Then answer Part B.

Part A Read this sentence from paragraph 5 again.

> It hurt me that she had been <u>put to shame</u> before the townspeople on my account, but she did not scold me.

What is the meaning of <u>put to shame</u> as the phrase is used in this sentence?

A angry

B scared

C impatient

D embarrassed

Part B Which detail from the text helps you understand the meaning of <u>put to shame</u>?

A my poor mother put up with some cutting remarks

B she did not scold me

C she suspected that there was some real reason

D Beaming with joy, I put it on

Question 3

Find *put to shame* in the passage and underline it. Then read the words and sentences around *put to shame* and look for clues about its meaning. In this sentence, it is the mother who is *put to shame*. Look for clues about something that was said or done to the mother and how it made her feel.

4. In "Earliest Recollections," what does the chart tell you about Albert Schweitzer that is not covered in the passage? Give at least two examples of what you can learn from the chart.

_____

_____

_____

_____

Question 4

Authors often use charts and graphs to provide additional information to the reader. What types of facts and details does the chart provide about Dr. Schweitzer?

STOP!

Read the passage. Then answer questions 1–10.

The Flower's Lesson

by Louisa May Alcott

"O sister," said the little rose bud, as she gazed at the sky,

"I wish that the Dew Elves, as they wander lightly by,

Would bring me a star; for they never grow dim,

The shining drops of dew the Elves bring each day

5   And place in my bosom, so soon pass away;

But a star would glitter brightly through the long summer hours,

And I should be fairer than all my sister flowers.

That were better far than the dew-drops that fall

On the high and the low, and come alike to all.

10   I would be fair and stately, with a bright star to shine

And give a queenly air to this crimson robe of mine."

And proudly she cried, "These fire-flies shall be

My jewels, since the stars can never come to me."

Just then a tiny dew-drop that hung o'er the dell

15   On the breast of the bud like a soft star fell;

But impatiently she flung it away from her leaf,

And it fell on her mother like a tear of grief,

While she folded to her breast, with wilful pride,

A glittering fire-fly that hung by her side.

20   "Heed," said the mother rose, "daughter mine,

continued →

Why shouldst thou seek for beauty not thine?

O my foolish little bud, do listen to thy mother;

Care only for true beauty, and seek for no other.

There will be grief and trouble in that wilful little heart;

25   Unfold thy leaves, my daughter, and let the fly depart."

But the proud little bud would have her own will,

And folded the fire-fly more closely still;

Till the struggling insect tore open the vest

Of purple and green, that covered her breast.

30   When the sun came up, she saw with grief

The blooming of her sister bud leaf by leaf.

While she, once as fair and bright as the rest,

Hung her weary head down on her wounded breast.

Bright grew the sunshine, and the soft summer air

35   Was filled with the music of flowers singing there;

But faint grew the little bud with thirst and pain,

And longed for the cool dew; but now't was in vain.

Then bitterly she wept for her folly and pride,

As drooping she stood by her fair sister's side.

40   Then from the mother's breast, where it still lay hid,

Into the fading bud the dew-drop gently slid;

Stronger grew the little form, and happy tears fell,

As the dew did its silent work, and the bud grew well,

While the gentle rose leaned, with motherly pride,

45   O'er the fair little ones that bloomed at her side.

Night came again, and the fire-flies flew;

But the bud let them pass, and drank of the dew.

Name_____ Date_____

1. This question has two parts. Answer Part A first. Then answer Part B.

Part A What did the bud want most of all at the beginning of the poem?

A to grow bigger than any other

B to drink the dew that fell on her

C to be more beautiful than her sisters

D to have stars shine and twinkle on her

Part B Which line from the poem supports the answer to Part A?

A And I should be fairer than all my sister flowers.

B Just then a tiny dew-drop that hung o'er the dell

C I would be fair and stately, with a bright star to shine

D But a star would glitter brightly through the long summer hours

2. Read the lines from the poem.

> There will be <u>grief</u> and trouble in that wilful little heart;
> Unfold thy leaves, my daughter, and let the fly depart.

What does the word <u>grief</u> mean as it is used in this poem?

A terror

B damage

C sadness

D nervousness

continued

Name_____ Date_____

3. This question has two parts. Answer Part A first. Then answer Part B.

Part A What is a theme of "The Flower's Lesson"?

A Love and support your sisters and mother.

B Always be the most beautiful of your kind.

C Share the treasures you have with others.

D Follow advice from those who have experience.

Part B Which line from the poem supports the answer to Part A?

A I would be fair and stately, with a bright star to shine

B O my foolish little bud, do listen to thy mother;

C But faint grew the little bud with thirst and pain,

D While the gentle rose leaned, with motherly pride,

4. Check the boxes of the lessons that can be learned from the poem "The Flower's Lesson."

❑   Be happy with who you are.

❑   Live and let live.

❑   Might makes right.

❑   Do not try to be something you are not.

❑   One good turn deserves another.

❑   Think before you act.

❑   There are two sides to every truth.

Name_____ Date_____

5. Read the lines from the poem. Decide which character is speaking, and check the correct box next to each line.

	The Bud	**The Mother**
But a star would glitter brightly through the long summer hours,		
Care only for true beauty, and seek for no other.		
And give a queenly air to this crimson robe of mine.		
That were better far than the dew-drops that fall		
There will be grief and trouble in that wilful little heart;		

6. To what does the poet compare the bud's petals?

A   a shirt

B   a vest

C   a jacket

D   a sweater

continued

Name_____ Date_____

7. Read these lines from the poem.

"<u>Heed</u>," said the mother rose, "daughter mine,

Why shouldst thou seek for beauty not thine?"

What does the word <u>heed</u> mean?

A stop it

B slow down

C look ahead

D pay attention

Name_____ Date_____

8. How does the reader know that the mother rose cares deeply for her bud? Use examples from the poem to support your answer.

_____

_____

_____

_____

_____

_____

9. Describe the way in which the bud got hurt. Use details from the poem to support your answer.

_____

_____

_____

_____

_____

continued

Name_____ Date_____

Common Core Reading Warm-Ups & Test Practice Grade 4 • ©2014 Newmark Learning, LLC

10. Retell the poem's story of the bud in three or four sentences. Use key details from the story in your retelling.

_____

_____

_____

_____

_____

_____

_____

_____

_____

_____

_____

_____

Read the passage. Then answer questions 1–10.

Amelia Earhart's Last Flight

from America's Library website, Library of Congress: www.americaslibrary.gov

1   After flying across the Atlantic as a passenger in 1928, Amelia
Earhart's next goal was to achieve a transatlantic crossing alone.
In 1927, Charles Lindbergh became the first person to make a solo
nonstop flight across the Atlantic. In 1932, exactly five years after
Lindbergh's flight, Earhart became the first woman to repeat the feat.
Her popularity grew even more. She was the undisputed queen of the
air! Still, she wanted to achieve more. What did Earhart do next?

2   She decided that her next trip would be to fly around the world. In
March 1937, she flew to Hawaii with fellow pilot Paul Mantz to begin
this flight. Earhart lost control of the plane on takeoff, however, and
the plane had to be sent to the factory for repairs.

continued ➤

3   In June, she went to Miami to again begin a flight around the world, this time with Fred Noonan as her navigator. No one knows why, but she left behind important communication and navigation instruments. Perhaps it was to make room for additional fuel for the long flight. The pair made it to New Guinea in 21 days, even though Earhart was tired and ill. During the next leg of the trip, they departed New Guinea for Howland Island, a tiny island in the middle of the Pacific Ocean. July 2, 1937, was the last time Earhart and Noonan communicated with a nearby Coast Guard ship. They were never heard from again. What do you think happened?

4   The U.S. Navy conducted a massive search for Earhart and Noonan that continued for more than two weeks. Unable to accept that Earhart had simply disappeared and perished, some of her admirers believed that she was a spy or was captured by enemies of the United States. The Navy submitted a report following its search, which included maps of search areas. Neither the plane nor Earhart nor Noonan were ever found. No one knows for sure what happened, but many people believe they got lost and simply ran out of fuel and died. Amelia Earhart was less than a month away from her 40th birthday.

5   No one knows if the sample will yield enough DNA for a proper test. If it does, then scientists will test it against the genetic material in the piece of bone. They will also compare it with DNA samples from Earhart's living relatives. The odds against such a match are long. After all, the bone might not be human at all. It may have come from the remains of a sea turtle found nearby.

Trying to Solve the Case

Amelia Earhart's plane disappeared over the Pacific in 1937. All that remained was a mystery—and, on an island near where Earhart disappeared, a bone fragment. The fragment was found during the search for Earhart and her plane. For years there was no way to be sure if this bone was even human. But DNA analysis has improved greatly in recent years. It may now be possible to find out if the bone does in fact belong to the famous flyer. To determine this, scientists are analyzing a sample of Earhart's saliva. The sample came from envelopes that Earhart licked, sealed, and sent many years ago.

continued

Name_____ Date_____

1. This question has two parts. Answer Part A first. Then answer Part B.

Part A What is the main idea of the sidebar, "Trying to Solve the Case"?

A   Science has made great progress in DNA research.

B   Scientists regard what happened to Amelia Earhart as a detective story.

C   Scientists plan to use DNA to match a bone fragment to Amelia Earhart.

D   A bone fragment thought to belong to Amelia Earhart may be from a turtle.

Part B Choose two sentences from the sidebar that support the answer to Part A.

A   Amelia Earhart's plane disappeared over the Pacific in 1937.

B   All that remained was a mystery—and, on an island near where Earhart disappeared, a bone fragment.

C   For years there was no way to be sure if this bone was even human.

D   But DNA analysis has improved greatly in recent years.

E   It may now be possible to find out if the bone does in fact belong to the famous flyer.

F   To determine this, scientists are analyzing a sample of Earhart's saliva.

Name_____ Date_____

2. This question has two parts. Answer Part A first. Then answer Part B.

Part A Read the sentence from the passage.

> If it does, then scientists will test it against the genetic material in the piece of bone.

What does the word genetic mean?

A made of chemicals

B found on an island

C taken from a sea turtle

D related to family background

Part B Which sentence from the sidebar helps you understand the meaning of the word genetic?

A The sample came from envelopes that Earhart licked, sealed, and sent many years ago.

B No one knows if the sample will yield enough DNA for a proper test.

C They will also compare it with DNA samples from Earhart's living relatives.

D After all, the bone might not be human at all.

continued

Name_____ Date_____

3. What structure does the author use to present most of the information in the passage?

A sequence of events

B comparison and contrast

C cause and effect

D order of importance

4. How does the author of the passage try to explain Amelia Earhart's disappearance? Check the box next to each sentence that gives an explanation.

☐ The U.S. Navy conducted a massive search for Earhart and Noonan that continued for more than two weeks.

☐ Unable to accept that Earhart had simply disappeared and perished, some of her admirers believed that she was a spy or was captured by enemies of the United States.

☐ The Navy submitted a report following its search, which included maps of search areas.

☐ Neither the plane nor Earhart nor Noonan were ever found.

☐ No one knows for sure what happened, but many people believe they got lost and simply ran out of fuel and died.

☐ Amelia Earhart was less than a month away from her 40th birthday.

Name_____ Date_____

5. What is the central idea of this passage?

A Amelia Earhart was the first woman to fly nonstop across the Atlantic Ocean by herself.

B Amelia Earhart disappeared in 1937 while trying to fly around the world, and no one knows what happened to her.

C Amelia Earhart crossed the Atlantic Ocean as a passenger in 1928, one year after Charles Lindbergh made the first nonstop solo crossing.

D Amelia Earhart and Fred Noonan left New Guinea on July 2, 1937, and were never heard from again.

6. Choose four sentences that belong in a summary of this passage and put them in correct order.

___ Earhart and her plane disappeared somewhere in the Pacific Ocean, and they were never found.

___ Scientists are now analyzing a bone fragment to see if it came from Amelia Earhart.

___ Amelia Earhart flew nonstop across the Atlantic Ocean in 1932.

___ When Earhart took off from Miami, she left behind some important equipment.

___ In 1937, she and Fred Noonan set off to fly around the world.

___ Amelia Earhart became famous for crossing the Atlantic Ocean as a passenger in an airplane.

continued

Name_____ Date_____

7. Choose three sentences to describe the steps in the process of trying to solve the mystery of what happened to Amelia Earhart. Then put them in correct order.

—   The science of DNA improves over several years.

—   Amelia Earhart's plane vanishes over the Pacific Ocean.

—   Scientists analyze the DNA sample to see if it can be matched to the bone fragment.

—   Scientists get a DNA sample of Earhart's saliva from old envelopes.

—   Amelia Earhart sends some letters in envelopes.

—   Searchers find a bone fragment on a Pacific Island near the place where Earhart disappeared.

—   The U.S. Navy submits a report about its search for Earhart's plane.

Name_____ Date_____

8. Why will it be difficult for scientists to prove that the bone fragment came from Amelia Earhart? Give at least two problems the scientists will face.

_____

_____

_____

_____

_____

_____

_____

9. How did Amelia Earhart become the "undisputed queen of the air"? Use details from the passage to support your answer.

_____

_____

_____

_____

_____

_____

_____

continued

Name_____ Date_____

10. Why is it important to find out if the bone fragment found on a Pacific Island came from Amelia Earhart? Use details from the passage to explain.

_____

_____

_____

_____

_____

_____

_____

_____

_____

_____

_____

_____

Read the passages. Then answer questions 1–10.

Small Rabbit's Long Nap

1   Small Rabbit lived in the woods with her family. In the warm months, many creatures were near the rabbit family's burrow—songbirds and mice and deer, to name a few. Small Rabbit loved the sounds and energy of these woodland neighbors.

2   Spring passed and summer passed. As autumn came and went, the weather grew cold. The songbirds flew to warmer places, taking their music with them; the mice and deer snuggled into hidden homes; and Small Rabbit scurried, lonesome, through the woods, listening for the busy sounds she loved. All was quiet but for her mother's call, beckoning her home to settle in for winter. So Small Rabbit headed reluctantly to the burrow, already impatient for spring.

continued ➤

3   Small Rabbit's family explained that they would have a long sleep until the warm days returned.

4   "A long sleep?" Small Rabbit grumped to her siblings. "I HATE naps," she told her father. He smiled and said, "You'll learn soon enough, Small Rabbit. Be patient."

5   Small Rabbit did not have any patience, and she was certain she did not want any, either. When her family fell asleep, she closed her eyes and pretended to sleep, too—but after a little while, she snuck out of the burrow, saying, "I'll just pick some tulips for Mother."

6   When Small Rabbit stepped outside, the whole wood looked frightening and different: the ground was covered in a cold, wet layer of white that stuck to her fur, and the icy wind made her shiver and shake. Perking her ears to listen for the sounds she loved, Small Rabbit was surprised to hear only something unfamiliar: "Who, who?" it seemed to ask. "Who, who-who?"

7   "Why, it's only me: Small Rabbit!" she called, surprised at the need to introduce herself. Everyone in the wood had always known her before.

8   A white owl, much larger than any of the birds she used to know, swooped to a low branch to meet her. "Well, Small Rabbit, it's a pleasure to know you. I don't mean to be rude, but I think you must be lost."

9   "L-L-Lost? But I live here!" Small Rabbit said, now shivering so much she could barely speak.

10   "I believe you live there," he smiled, gesturing toward her burrow. "It's far too cold out here. My feathers keep me warm, but you smaller creatures must squeeze close to your families to survive the winter; you'll never make it alone."

11 "B-But I don't like naps." Yet Small Rabbit, so overwhelmed by the cold, was suddenly quite interested in the idea of snuggling with her family. "W-W-Well, I sup-p-p-pose I could try it out, though. It's only that I c-c-can't wait for spring to come."

12 Parting with the owl, Small Rabbit shivered her way back to the burrow; she was cold and wet and sleepy. Squeezing between her siblings for warmth, she shut her eyes, thinking, "A little nap can't hurt if I have to wait inside anyway."

13 By the time she awoke, spring had come—songbirds, tulips, and all.

continued

The Lost Surprise

1   It was the week before my tenth birthday, and I was anxiously awaiting the arrival of my special day. My younger brother, Pablo, seemed almost as excited to celebrate this birthday as I was.

2   "Maria," Pablo whispered, "I think Mama is making pan dulce for your birthday breakfast, and a flan for birthday dessert!"

3   With thoughts of sweet bread and soft, pudding-like cake whirling in my mind, I was excited enough; but as the day neared, Pablo told me more things.

4   "The neighbors will come to the party! And I saw Mama wrapping a big present for you—it's hidden in the hall closet!"

5   "Hush, Pablo; it's supposed to be a surprise!" I said, struggling to mask the eagerness in my voice.

6   The day before my birthday, I thought I might burst with excitement.

7   "Mama," I pleaded, "may I open my present early? I can't wait any longer!"

8   "Patience, Maria. The surprise is the best part."

9   "Oh, Mama," I complained—but I knew I couldn't persuade her.

10   "Go practice your violin, Maria."

11   My skin prickled for a moment: my violin case was in the hall closet, right where Pablo had said my secret birthday gift was hidden! Seeing that my mother was outside, away from view, I let myself sneak a tiny look at the gift, which was tucked behind a suitcase.

12   "What a funny shape!" I whispered, itching with curiosity. "I'll just take a little peek."

13   I tucked my finger under a bit of tape and lifted the yellow wrapping paper. Through the little corner I'd undone, I could see only a bit of color.

14   "Just a little more," I told myself, "since this is hardly enough of a look!"

15   I worked gradually, opening corner after corner, and before I knew it, I'd unwrapped the entire thing to reveal a beautiful piñata, a Mexican party gift. It was shaped like a horse—my favorite animal—and covered in brightly colored paper. The most special thing about a piñata is that there are treats hidden inside. I'd never had my very own piñata, and I was eager to share it with my friends and break it open. Beaming, I touched the gift and giggled a little.

16   "Maria," my mother called from outside. I jumped with surprise. A dark feeling of shame and embarrassment crept into my stomach. "Maria, practice your violin, please!"

17   That night, I carefully rewrapped the piñata in new paper and returned it to its place behind the suitcase. Practicing my "surprised" face in the mirror, I regretted that I hadn't waited, and that my mother hadn't seen my genuine, delighted reaction.

18   My birthday was lovely: pan dulce for breakfast; chicken tostadas, flan, and fresh fruit for lunch; and even sugary churros that Pablo had successfully kept secret. When my friends and I played with the piñata, we found wonderful treats inside, just as I'd hoped. But I knew, for next year, that it is always more fun to wait. I'd missed the best part—the surprise—and it wasn't nearly worth the trade.

continued

Name_____ Date_____

1. Read this sentence from the passage "Small Rabbit's Long Nap."

> All was quiet but for her mother's call, <u>beckoning</u> her home to settle in for winter.

Which word means the same as <u>beckoning</u>?

A calling

B asking

C moving

D sending

2. Why is Small Rabbit afraid when she leaves her family's burrow?

A because it is dark

B because she is alone

C because she becomes lost

D because everything looks different

Name_____ Date_____

3. This question has two parts. Answer Part A first. Then answer Part B.

Part A Which word **best** describes the white owl?

A scary

B kind

C comical

D mysterious

Part B Which sentence from the passage best supports the answer to Part A?

A "Who, who?" it seemed to ask. "Who, who-who?"

B "Well, Small Rabbit, it's a pleasure to know you. I don't mean to be rude, but I think you must be lost."

C A white owl, much larger than any of the birds she used to know, swooped to a low branch to meet her.

D Parting with the owl, Small Rabbit shivered her way back to the burrow; she was cold and wet and sleepy.

continued ➤

Name_____ Date_____

4. This question has two parts. Answer Part A first. Then answer Part B.

Part A How does Maria feel after Pablo tells her about what is hidden in the closet?

A upset

B excited

C indifferent

D disappointed

Part B Which line of dialogue from the passage supports the answer to Part A?

A "The neighbors will come to the party! And I saw Mama wrapping a big present for you—it's hidden in the hall closet!"

B "Hush, Pablo; it's supposed to be a surprise!" I said, struggling to mask the eagerness in my voice.

C "Patience, Maria. The surprise is the best part."

D "What a funny shape!" I whispered, itching with curiosity. "I'll just take a little peek."

Name_____ Date_____

5. Which five statements belong in a summary of the passage "The Lost Surprise"? Choose the five sentences and number them in the correct order.

—   Maria had never had her own piñata before.

—   Maria's mother tells her to be patient.

—   Pablo tells Maria that he saw their mother wrapping her present.

—   Maria decides that next year she will not spoil her birthday surprise.

—   Maria ate pan dulce for breakfast.

—   Maria asks her mother if she can open her present early.

—   The piñata was filled with treats.

—   Maria unwraps her present to find out what it is and then rewraps it.

—   The piñata was shaped like a horse.

continued

Name_____ Date_____

6. Read this sentence from the passage "The Lost Surprise."

Practicing my "surprised" face in the mirror, I regretted that I hadn't waited, and that my mother hadn't seen my <u>genuine</u>, delighted reaction.

Which word means almost the same thing as <u>genuine</u> as it is used in the passage?

A fake

B happy

C natural

D surprised

Name_____ Date_____

7. If "Small Rabbit's Long Nap" was rewritten as a play, which three elements would be added? Check the box next to each the element that you choose.

☐ cast of characters

☐ dialogue

☐ stanzas

☐ plot

☐ stage directions

☐ verses

☐ scenes or acts

continued

Name_____ Date_____

8. Describe the setting of "Small Rabbit's Long Nap." Use details from the
passage to support your answer.

_____

_____

_____

_____

_____

_____

_____

_____

Name_____ Date_____

9. Compare and contrast how Maria feels at the beginning of the story to how she feels at the end of the story. Use details from the story to support your answer.

_____

_____

_____

_____

_____

_____

_____

_____

continued

Name_____ Date_____

10. Both Small Rabbit in "Small Rabbit's Long Nap" and Maria in "The Lost Surprise" make a choice they regret. Compare how these characters respond to their poor choice. Use details from each passage to support your answer.

_____

_____

_____

_____

_____

_____

_____

_____

_____

_____

_____

_____

STOP!

Read the passages. Then answer questions 1–10.

A Fire for Liberty

1   Rebecca Brewton Motte was the daughter of a wealthy merchant in Charleston, South Carolina. As a young woman, Rebecca married Jacob Motte. Her husband supported the colonists' efforts to break free from Great Britain. When the Revolutionary War started, Rebecca was an eager supporter of the American patriot cause, too.

2   In 1780, British forces took over the city of Charleston, which was not good news for Rebecca. Things went from bad to worse when officers of the British army decided to make their headquarters at the Brewton House, where Rebecca and her family lived. Rebecca spent her days attending to her husband, who was very ill, as well as feeding the British soldiers who were staying in her house. Still, this situation did not stop Rebecca from aiding the American forces. She made arrangements to secretly send corn, rice, and pork to the hungry American troops. Not long after, Rebecca's husband died; she then received permission from the British to take her daughters to the family home known as Buckhead, which was outside the city.

continued

3   Rebecca and her daughters had been at Buckhead for only a few months when the British came knocking again. The American troops were on the move toward Charleston, and the British intended to avoid their arrival. The British soldiers dug a huge trench around Rebecca's property. Then, they cut down many of the beautiful trees to build a barrier around the house, which became known as "Fort Motte." Rebecca and her children were sent to live in a small farmhouse.

4   The Americans were determined to defeat the British and overtake Fort Motte. One of the American leaders, Francis Marion, visited Rebecca. He explained to her that it was vital to the American cause to defeat the British. Unfortunately, the only way the Americans could succeed in their victory was to burn down Rebecca's much-loved house. But if Rebecca had any regrets about losing her home, she kept them to herself. She told Marion she understood and gave him her permission. Not only that, but she also gave Marion a bow that had belonged to her brother, along with some arrows, to use to set the fire. Even though Rebecca had many happy memories of her house, the cause of freedom for the American colonies was far more important to her.

5   The American patriots used Rebecca's gift and succeeded in setting fire to the roof of Buckhead. The fire forced the British soldiers to evacuate the house, and American soldiers were waiting to capture them. Happily, the fire was put out before it completely destroyed the Motte house. That evening, Rebecca prepared dinner for both the American soldiers and the British officers that had been captured. Today, Rebecca Brewton Motte is remembered as one of many female patriots who helped the Americans in their struggle for freedom.

Sybil Ludington's Ride

1   Sybil Ludington has been called the "female Paul Revere" and a "Revolutionary War hero." Like Revere, she made a difficult ride on horseback to warn American forces about the approach of British troops. Her actions helped the colonists win the American Revolution.

2   Sybil Ludington was born in 1761 on the New York-Connecticut border. The oldest of twelve children, she grew up in Kent, New York. Sybil's father was Colonel Henry Ludington, a farmer and mill operator. He fought with the British in the French and Indian War, which ended in 1763. By 1773, he had joined the American cause against England and had formed a volunteer militia in his area. According to some stories, Henry Ludington also oversaw spies who kept an eye on the British.

3   One night in the spring of 1777, a messenger arrived at the Ludington household with news of a British attack on Danbury, Connecticut. The British had set fire to some private homes and colonial army storehouses. American leaders needed Henry Ludington to muster his volunteer militia to fight the British.

continued

4   But there was a problem: the men had disbanded and returned to their farms for the planting season. They were scattered all over the county. The messenger was too exhausted to ride out and gather those men. Henry Ludington had to stay at the farm to get everything ready for the militia. So he asked his daughter Sybil to rally the troops in his place.

5   Sybil agreed. At 9:00 P.M. that night, rain was falling when she left the family farm. Sybil's ride took her on rough roads through rugged countryside and dark woods. She had to watch out for roughnecks and outlaws along the way. She also had to avoid British sympathizers. They would try to stop her and put her in jail so she could not get word to the troops. Sybil rode more than forty miles through the night and returned home the next day.

6   Her ride was a success. Most members of her father's militia arrived at the farmhouse by dawn, ready to fight the British.

7   In the weeks that followed, neighbors and friends thanked Sybil for her bravery. Even George Washington traveled to the Ludington homestead to express his gratitude.

8   Sybil's ride never received the widespread recognition of Paul Revere's, yet her trip was nearly twice as long. Still, Ludington's amazing efforts have been acknowledged in many ways. Poems have been written about her daring. Several books document her story. An artist named Anna Hyatt Huntington made a statue of Sybil on her horse. New York State set up markers to show her route. And in 1975, nearly 200 years after her remarkable ride, the U.S. Congress honored Sybil Ludington with a postage stamp.

Name_____ Date_____

1. This question has two parts. Answer Part A first. Then answer Part B.

Part A In the passage "A Fire for Liberty," how did Rebecca Brewton Motte react when the British army made her home, the Brewton House, their headquarters?

A She burned the house down.

B She moved into a new home.

C She decided to support the British cause.

D She continued to aid the American forces.

Part B Which sentence from the passage supports the answer to Part A?

A She made arrangements to secretly send corn, rice, and pork to the hungry American troops.

B The American troops were on the move toward Charleston, and the British intended to avoid their arrival.

C Rebecca spent her days attending to her husband, who was very ill, as well as feeding the British soldiers who were staying in her house.

D Not long after, Rebecca's husband died; she then received permission from the British to take her daughters to the family home known as Buckhead, which was outside the city.

continued

Name_____ Date_____

2. What is the main idea of the passage "A Fire for Liberty"?

A British troops allowed Rebecca Brewton Motte to leave her home after they turned it into a fortress.

B The American forces could not have won the Revolutionary War without help from ordinary people.

C Rebecca Brewton Motte made sacrifices to help the American patriots win the Revolutionary War.

D British forces took over the city of Charleston, South Carolina in 1780, but were eventually defeated.

3. Choose six sentences that should be included in a summary of "A Fire for Liberty." Number them in the correct order.

—   Rebecca moved with her daughters to her home Buckhead.

—   The American patriots asked Rebecca for permission to burn her family's home to get the British out.

—   The British soldiers took over Buckhead and turned it into a fort.

—   Rebecca gave Francis Marion the bow that belonged to her brother.

—   The American patriots set fire to the roof of Buckhead and captured the British soldiers.

—   The British forces took over the city of Charleston, South Carolina and made their headquarters in Rebecca's home.

—   Rebecca took care of her sick husband.

—   Rebecca secretly sent food to the American soldiers when the British troops were living in her house.

—   The British cut down the trees around Rebecca's house and called it Fort Motte.

Name_____ Date_____

4. Read this sentence from the passage "Sybil Ludington's Ride."

> American leaders needed Henry Ludington to <u>muster</u> his volunteer militia to fight the British.

Which word means almost the same as <u>muster</u> as it is used in the passage?

A help

B fight

C meet

D gather

5. This question has two parts. Answer Part A first. Then answer Part B.

Part A According to the passage "Sybil Ludington's Ride," why did Henry Ludington ask his daughter to rally the troops in his place?

A He was too tired to go himself.

B She was the best horseback rider in town.

C He had to stay and get his farm ready for the militia.

D No one else knew where to find the militia members.

Part B Which paragraph provides support for the answer to Part A?

A paragraph 3

B paragraph 4

C paragraph 5

D paragraph 6

continued ➡

Name_____ Date_____

6. Choose three details from the passage to support the idea that Sybil Ludington faced many dangers on her ride. Check the box next to each detail you choose.

☐ But there was a problem: the men had disbanded and returned to their farms for the planting season.

☐ They were scattered all over the county.

☐ At 9:00 P.M. that night, rain was falling when she left the family farm.

☐ Sybil's ride took her on rough roads through rugged countryside and dark woods.

☐ She had to watch out for roughnecks and outlaws along the way.

☐ She also had to avoid British sympathizers.

☐ Sybil rode more than forty miles through the night and returned home the next day.

7. Based on the information presented in the passages, what did Rebecca Brewton Motte and Sybil Ludington have in common?

A They both lived in New England.

B They both lived with their father.

C They both sent food to American troops.

D They both supported the Americans during the American Revolution.

Name_____ Date_____

Common Core Reading Warm-Ups & Test Practice Grade 4 • ©2014 Newmark Learning, LLC

8. Read this sentence from the conclusion of "A Fire for Liberty."

> Today, Rebecca Brewton Motte is remembered as one of many female patriots who helped the Americans in their struggle for freedom.

What evidence does the author present to support this statement? Use details from the passage to support your answer.

_____

_____

_____

_____

_____

_____

_____

continued

Name_____ Date_____

9. Read these sentences from the first paragraph of "Sybil Ludington's Ride."

Sybil Ludington has been called the "female Paul Revere" and a "Revolutionary War hero." Like Revere, she made a difficult ride on horseback to warn American forces about the approach of British troops.

How does the author support the claim that Sybil Ludington's ride was difficult? Use details from the passage to support your answer.

_____

_____

_____

_____

_____

_____

_____

Name_____ Date_____

10. Compare and contrast the ways that Rebecca Brewton Motte and Sybil Ludington worked to help the American patriots during the Revolutionary War. Use details from the passages to support your answer.

_____

_____

_____

_____

_____

_____

_____

_____

_____

_____

_____

_____

_____

The Art of Mistakes • Warm Up 1

Question & Answer	Standards
1. Which word best describes how Kelly feels at each point in the story? Choose the feeling word that matches each sentence from the passage. Write the word in the correct box. <table><tr><td>**Detail**</td><td>**Feelings**</td></tr><tr><td>Kelly raced down the hallway to the classroom.</td><td>**excited**</td></tr><tr><td>A peal of thunder made Kelly jump, which caused her paintbrush to drag across the canvas.</td><td>**surprised**</td></tr><tr><td>As she struggled to clean up her mess, she realized she had only succeeded in spreading the multicolored splotches around, ruining her painting.</td><td>**upset**</td></tr><tr><td>Kelly grinned and said, "Oops."</td><td>**happy**</td></tr></table>	RL.4.3
2. Identify the statements from the text that help describe the setting. Place a check in the box next to each statement you choose. ❏ She dreamt of doodling day and night, planning her next creation in her mind. ❏ Kelly raced down the hallway to the classroom. ❏ She slipped into an apron to cover her clothes and sat down on a sturdy stool. ❏ Kelly knew that if she flicked her wrist just right, she could make the paint look like grass. ❏ **She added some flowers before moving on to the sky: a brilliant blue filled with white puffy clouds.** ❏ As she struggled to clean up her mess, she realized she had only succeeded in spreading the multicolored splotches around, ruining her painting. ❏ **She was so involved in painting that she didn't notice the rainstorm that began pelting the windows.** ❏ Thinking quickly, Mr. Jacobs rubbed his chin thoughtfully and nodded his head.	RL.4.3
3 Part A. This question has two parts. Answer Part A first. Then answer Part B. Read this sentence from the passage: She was so <u>involved in</u> the painting that she didn't notice the rainstorm that began pelting the windows." What is the meaning of <u>involved in</u>, as it is used in this sentence? A tired of B bothered by C disappointed in D **working hard on**	RL.4.4
3 Part B. Which phrase helps you understand the meaning of involved in? A Not one to panic B fix her mistake C **she didn't notice the rainstorm** D which caused her paintbrush to drag	RL.4.1, RL.4.4

The Start of Something New • Warm Up 2

Question & Answer	Standards
1. Read this sentence from the passage. How is it that today's art museums feature so many different styles? Many say it all began with a group of men and women called the Impressionists. Select the details the author uses to support this idea. Check the box next to each statement you choose. ❑ This insult effectively named the movement. ❑ **Impressionism opened the doors for other artists to try new creative styles.** ❑ **The Impressionists' breathtaking artwork taught critics that there were more things worth painting than royalty and religion.** ❑ Some Impressionists, like Pierre-Auguste Renoir and Claude Monet, spent years studying one subject alone, like dancers or water lilies. ❑ **Unlike the other artists of their time, these painters used surprising colors; vague, blurry shapes; and hurried-looking brushstrokes to represent the objects they painted.** ❑ They painted the same things repeatedly, in different lights and colors, highlighting motion and feeling. ❑ **Today, there is no "correct" way of painting.** ❑ Many Impressionists lived in poverty because their paintings did not sell well.	**RI.4.8**
2. Which detail from the text supports the inference that today people admire and value the work of the Impressionists? A **They knew their work was beautiful and important.** B These artists captured the vibrancy of life as no one had before. C Today, their costly paintings hang in the world's greatest museums. D People were slow to like the artwork	**RI.4.1**
3. Read this sentence from the passage: This art sought to look realistic and the subjects were always <u>religious</u> or historic. What is the meaning of <u>religious</u> as it is used in this sentence? A like a photograph B **having to do with God** C about the royal family D important to French people	**RI.4.4**

Don't Give Up • Warm Up 3

Question & Answer	Standards
1. What is the theme of the poem? A winning B **keep trying** C learning to fly D not taking risks	**RL.4.2**
2. What does the phrase <u>gaining victory from defeat</u> mean in this poem? A to earn a prize B to fail an easy test C **to succeed after failing** D to win against a losing team	**RL.4.4**
3. Match each detail listed below with the correct stanza in the poem. Write the stanza number (1, 2, 3, or 4) in the box next to each detail. If a detail applies to more than one stanza, write each correct number in the box.	**RL.4.5**

Details	Stanza
Lines one and three rhyme.	1, 3, and 4
Birds get stronger each time they try to fly.	2
You should not waste time feeling sorry for yourself.	1
Lines two and four rhyme.	1, 2, 3, and 4
It is best to succeed doing something difficult.	4
The oak tree grew taller after winds bowed it.	3
Great things happen when people don't give up.	1

Swimming • Warm Up 4

Question & Answer	Standards
1 Part A. This question has two parts. Answer Part A first. Then answer Part B. What is the main idea of "Swimming"? A the correct way to move your arms in water B **ways to keep your head above water** C where to sign up for swimming lessons D how to get help in a swimming emergency	RI.4.2
1 Part B. Which detail from the text supports the answer to Part A? A Swimming is more than a great way to cool off when it's hot. B While you're moving your legs, sweep your arms together with your palms facing down and in. C **Another way to keep afloat is to tread water.** D If you don't know how to swim, or if you want to brush up your skills, you'll want to take some lessons at your local pool.	RI.4.1
2. What is the meaning of the phrase <u>brush up</u> in paragraph 1? A to scrub or polish B **to practice** C to clean D to learn	RI.4.4
3. Read each description and decide whether it applies to floating or treading water. Write the letter in the correct column.	RI.4.3

Floating	Treading Water
A arch your back	**C** pretend you are riding a bicycle
B let the water support your body	**E** keep your back straight
D kick your legs gently	**G** sweep your arms together and back out
F stretch your arms out to the side	
H take short breaths	

from "Gareth and Lynette" • Warm Up 5

Question & Answer	Standards
1 Part A. This question has two parts. Answer Part A first. Then answer Part B. What inference can you make from the passage? A The queen worried that Gareth would get hurt while playing in the forest. B The queen did not love her other sons as much as she loved Gareth. C Gareth wanted to join King Arthur's court to be with his brothers. D **Gareth told his mother about his adventures because he had no friends and his father could not hear well and did not speak.**	**RL.4.1**
1 Part B. Which detail from the story supports the answer to Part A? A She was afraid that some day, when Gareth was older, he would want to leave her to go into the world, perhaps to go to the great King Arthur's court, as his three brothers had done. B **Gareth had no little boys or girls to play with, for there were no houses near his mountain home.** C Sometimes the birds and beasts, his woodland friends, would call to him, and then Gareth would wander about in the forest with them till evening came. D Then he would follow them up the mountains, till he found the place where the streams ended in tiny silver threads.	**RL.4.1**
2. If this story were turned into a play, which new elements would be added? character development **dialogue** **a cast of characters** **stage directions** stanzas **acts or scenes** a setting	**RL.4.5**
3. Which of the descriptions below best fit the character Gareth and which best fit the queen? Choose four descriptions for each character and write the letters below the character's name. | Gareth	The Queen
B never bored	**A** adventurous
C unhappy	**E** entertaining
D cheerful	**G** loves nature
F worried	**H** does not want to be alone		**RL.4.3**

Special Quarters • Warm Up 6

Question & Answer	Standards
1 Part A. This question has two parts. Answer Part A first. Then answer Part B. What is the main idea of the passage? A why the quarter was created B how to start a quarter collection C why Washington is on the quarter D **how quarters have changed over time**	**RI.4.2**
1 Part B. Which detail from the passage supports the answer to Part A? A **The next change to the design of the quarter came in 1999.** B The program was created to encourage a new generation of coin collectors. C The U.S. quarter dollar (commonly known as "the quarter") has been produced since 1796. D The U.S. government made a profit of more than $3 billion from people who collected the coins, taking them out of circulation.	**RI.4.1, RI.4.2**
2. Based on the passage, choose the cause of each effect listed. Draw a line connecting each cause to its effect. **Cause** Half of Americans collected the 50 State Quarters. The 50 State Quarters program was created. The America the Beautiful Quarters program was created. **Effect** Fifty-six new quarters will have been released by 2021. The U.S. government made more than $3 billion. New people became interested in coin collecting.	**RI.4.3**
3. Use the text and the chart to determine which statements are correct. Check the box next to each statement you choose. ❏ **The America the Beautiful Quarters program is to run from 2010 until 2021.** ❏ **Five quarters will be released each year.** ❏ Grand Canyon National Park was featured in 2011. ❏ **The front of each quarter will have a portrait of George Washington.** ❏ U.S. territories will not be included in the America the Beautiful Quarters program. ❏ **A total of 56 America the Beautiful Quarters will be released.** ❏ The America the Beautiful Quarters from Alabama is already available. ❏ Mt. Hood National Forest is in Puerto Rico. ❏ **The first design in 2011 featured Gettysburg National Military Park.** ❏ **Acadia National Park is in Maine.**	**RI.4.7**

108

Question & Answer	Standards
4. Why do you think the U.S. Mint started the America the Beautiful Quarters program? Use details from the text to support your answer. **Sample answer:** The U.S. Mint started the America the Beautiful Quarters program because the 50 States Quarters program was so successful. The program made the government $3 billion and half the population collected the coins.	RI.4.1

A Golden Riddle • Warm Up 7

Question & Answer	Standards
1 Part A. This is a two-part question. Answer Part A first. Then answer Part B. Which statement is a theme of "A Golden Riddle"? A Fear can make people fail. B Taking risks is often dangerous. C Wealth makes people powerful. D **Knowledge is more important than strength.**	**RL.4.2**
1 Part B. Which detail from the text supports the answer to Part A? A The knight was stumped; everyone knows that dragons love gold more than any person or any thing. B The dragon growled, fire escaping from his mouth. C **"I will give you back the gold if you can solve my riddle; but if you cannot, I get to keep the chest of gold."** D "Finders keepers," rumbled the dragon.	**RL.4.2**
2. Which of the following can you infer from the text? A **The knight is loyal to his queen.** B The queen is afraid of dragons. C The cave is not far from the castle. D The dragon will steal the gold back.	**RL.4.1**
3. Choose a trait to describe each character in the story. Write the letter next to the character's name in the Trait column. Then choose an action that reveals that trait. Write the letter next to the character's name in the Action column. **Character Traits** **Character Actions** A. commanding E. solved a riddle B. fearful F. showed sharp teeth C. fierce G. gave an order D. clever H. paced the floor <table><tr><th>Character</th><th>Trait</th><th>Action</th></tr><tr><td>Dragon</td><td>C</td><td>F</td></tr><tr><td>Knight</td><td>D</td><td>E</td></tr><tr><td>Queen</td><td>A</td><td>G</td></tr></table>	**RL.4.3**
4. Write a summary of "A Golden Riddle" in your own words. **Sample answer:** In the story "A Golden Riddle," the queen's gold is stolen and she sends a knight to get it back. When the knight finds the gold with a dragon, the dragon challenges him to answer a riddle to get the gold back. The knight correctly answers the riddle and is able to retrieve the gold.	**RL.4.2**

Our Friend the Bat • Warm Up 8

Question & Answer	Standards
1 Part A. This question has two parts. Answer Part A first. Then answer Part B. What is the main idea of "Our Friend the Bat"? A Bats make excellent pets. B **Bats are interesting animals.** C Bats eat many different things. D Bats are dangerous to humans.	**RI.4.2**
1 Part B. Which detail from the passage supports the answer to Part A? A Some people put up special houses for bats. B Many people are frightened of bats, but unnecessarily so. C **Bats are among the world's most interesting and amazing creatures.** D The diet of a bat is varied, ranging from insects to fruit to small animals such as mice and birds.	**RI.4.1**
2. How is the information in this passage organized? A Each paragraph focuses on a different type of bat. B Each paragraph explains a different myth about bats. C **Each paragraph discusses a different topic related to bats.** D Each paragraph describes a different way bats are helpful.	**RI.4.5**
3. Which of the following inferences can you make from the passage "Our Friend the Bat"? Place a checkmark in the box next to each statement you choose. ❏ Bats carry germs. ❏ The author is scared of bats. ❏ **The author thinks bats have been unfairly judged.** ❏ **The earth needs bats.** ❏ Bats keep our water clean. ❏ **The author likes bats.** ❏ Some people keep bats as pets. ❏ Bats compete with humans for food.	**RI.4.1**
4. What is the author's point of view on the role of bats in the environment? What two details does the author use to support this point of view? **Sample answer:** The author's point of view is that bats are an important part of a healthy environment. The author states that bats help farmers by eating insects. The author also mentions that bats eat mosquitos, and help pollinate plants.	**RI.4.8**

Falling into Place • Warm Up 9

Question & Answer	Standards
1 Part A. This question has two parts. Answer Part A first. Then answer Part B. What inference can you make about Angela from the beginning of "Falling into Place"? A She is a showoff. B **She wants to fit in.** C She makes new friends easily. D She likes black better than red.	**RL.4.1**
1 Part B. Which sentence from the passage supports the answer to Part A? A She had left her new red sneakers in her bedroom closet. B On the way into school, Angela smiled at some girls from her class. C **Everybody at Angela's new school seemed to be wearing black-and-white sneakers.** D "I could show you a few tricks my mom taught me," Angela said, as Lucy and Mike pulled their chairs up to her desk.	**RL.4.1**
2. Choose five sentences that should be included in a summary of "Falling into Place." Number them in the correct order. Mike and Lucy ask Angela about her drawing. **[4]** Angela put on her black-and-white sneakers. Angela's mom tells her to be herself and everything will work out. **[2]** Angela offers to help Lucy and Mike learn to draw. **[5]** Angela should have introduced herself to her classmates. Because she doesn't have anyone to talk to, Angela begins drawing at her desk. **[3]** Angela is having a hard time because she is going to a new school. **[1]** Angela's mother sat next to her on the porch.	**RL.4.2**
3. Which details from the text support the inference that Angela's mother understands how Angela feels? Check the box next to each detail you choose. ❑ "Why are you wearing your old sneakers?" ❑ She was embarrassed to admit the truth to her mother. ❑ **Without pushing for more information, Angela's mother stood up and headed for the car.** ❑ **"Just be yourself, and everything will fall into place."** ❑ A few minutes later, they arrived at Keystone Middle School. ❑ Angela's mom sat down next to her. ❑ "My mom's an art teacher," Angela explained.	**RL.4.1**

Question & Answer	Standards
4. In "Falling into Place," why did Angela start drawing a picture at her desk, and what happened as a result? **Sample answer:** Everyone else in the classroom was occupied, and Angela had no one to talk to. She remembered her mother's advice to be herself, so she started drawing. Drawing helped her relax and relieve her worries. It also attracted the attention of two classmates, who came over and joined her.	**RL.4.3**

Earliest Recollections • Warm Up 10

Question & Answer	Standards
1. Which of the following inferences can you make from this passage? Check the box next to each inference you choose. ❏ **Albert is not proud of being the parson's son.** ❏ **The village boys come from poor families.** ❏ Albert thinks he is better than the village boys. ❏ Albert's parents want him to dress up for church. ❏ George Nitschelm gets in a lot of fights. ❏ **Albert would rather have friends than nice clothes.** ❏ Albert does not like going to church. ❏ Mother does not like the village boys.	RI.4.1
2. In paragraph 2, what does the author mean when he says "it cost me a big effort to keep back the tears." A It would take a lot of money for him to cry. B **It was hard for him not to cry.** C It was hard work to cry. D It was difficult for him to cry.	RI.4.4
3 Part A. This question has two parts. Answer Part A first. Then answer Part B. Read this sentence from paragraph 5 again. It hurt me that she had been <u>put to shame</u> before the townspeople on my account, but she did not scold me. What is the meaning of <u>put to shame</u> as the phrase is used in this sentence? A angry B scared C impatient D **embarrassed**	RI.4.4
3 Part B. Which detail from the text helps you understand the meaning of put to shame? A **my poor mother put up with some cutting remarks** B she did not scold me C she suspected that there was some real reason D Beaming with joy, I put it on	RI.4.4
4. In "Earliest Recollections," what does the chart tell you about Albert Schweitzer that is not covered in the passage? Give at least two examples of what you can learn from the chart. **Sample answer:** The chart gives information about Albert Schweitzer's career and accomplishments. It tells what he did for work. He was a doctor and an author. It also tells of awards he won, such as the Nobel Peace Prize.	RI.4.7

The Flower's Lesson • Practice Test 1

Question & Answer	Standards
1 Part A. This question has two parts. Answer Part A first. Then answer Part B. What did the bud want most of all at the beginning of the poem? A to grow bigger than any other B to drink the dew that fell on her C **to be more beautiful than her sisters** D to have stars shine and twinkle on her	RL.4.1
1 Part B. Which line from the poem supports the answer to Part A? A **And I should be fairer than all my sister flowers.** B Just then a tiny dew-drop that hung o'er the dell C I would be fair and stately, with a bright star to shine D But a star would glitter brightly through the long summer hours,	RL.4.1
2. Read the lines from the poem. There will be <u>grief</u> and trouble in that wilful little heart; Unfold thy leaves, my daughter, and let the fly depart." What does the word <u>grief</u> mean as it is used in this poem? A terror B damage C **sadness** D nervousness	RL.4.4
3 Part A. This question has two parts. Answer Part A first. Then answer Part B. What is a theme of "The Flower's Lesson"? A Love and support your sisters and mother. B Always be the most beautiful of your kind. C Share the treasures you have with others. D **Follow advice from those who have experience.**	RL.4.2
3 Part B. Which line from the poem supports the answer to Part A? A I would be fair and stately, with a bright star to shine B **O my foolish little bud, do listen to thy mother;** C But faint grew the little bud with thirst and pain, D While the gentle rose leaned, with motherly pride,	RL.4.2
4. Check the boxes of the lessons that can be learned from the poem, "The Flower's Lesson." ❏ **Be happy with who you are.** ❏ Live and let live. ❏ Might makes right. ❏ **Do not try to be something you are not.** ❏ One good turn deserves another. ❏ **Think before you act.** ❏ There are two sides to every truth.	RL.4.2

Question & Answer	Standards
5. Read the lines from the poem. Decide which character is speaking, and check the correct box next to each line. <table><tr><td></td><td>**The Bud**</td><td>**The Mother**</td></tr><tr><td>But a star would glitter brightly through the long summer hours,</td><td>✔</td><td></td></tr><tr><td>Care only for true beauty, and seek for no other.</td><td></td><td>✔</td></tr><tr><td>And give a queenly air to this crimson robe of mine.</td><td>✔</td><td></td></tr><tr><td>That were better far than the dew-drops that fall</td><td>✔</td><td></td></tr><tr><td>There will be grief and trouble in that wilful little heart;</td><td></td><td>✔</td></tr></table>	**RL.4.1**
6. To what does the poet compare the bud's petals? A a shirt B **a vest** C a jacket D a sweater	**RL.4.1**
7. Read these lines from the poem. "<u>Heed</u>," said the mother rose, "daughter mine, Why shouldst thou seek for beauty not thine?" What does the word <u>heed</u> mean? A stop it B slow down C look ahead D **pay attention**	**RL.4.4**
8. How does the reader know that the mother rose cares deeply for her bud? Use examples from the poem to support your answer. **Sample answer:** The bud's mother tries to stop her from catching the fire-fly. She tells her that unless she starts listening to others' advice, "There will be grief and trouble in that wilful little heart." Once the bud's petals are torn, her mother saves her by giving her back the dew-drop that the bud had flung away earlier. It is only because her mother saved the drop that the young bud survives.	**RL.4.3**
9. Describe the way in which the bud got hurt. Use details from the poem to support your answer. **Sample answer:** The bud wanted to shine like a star, so she caught a fire-fly in her petals. She thought that if she held the fire-fly, she would glow like a star. But the fire-fly was scared and wanted to get out, so it fought and tore her petals.	**RL.4.3**

Question & Answer	Standards
10. Retell the poem's story of the bud in three or four sentences. Use key details from the story in your retelling. **Sample answer:** A rose bud wants to be more beautiful than her sisters, so she ignores her mother's warning and catches a glowing fire-fly in her petals. Her mother tells her to let it go because she was not meant to glow, just to be a beautiful flower. The fire-fly tears the bud's petals to escape, so the bud cannot bloom like her sisters do. She is sad and in pain until her mother gives her a drop of dew to drink. She grows stronger, blooms, and never again wishes to be something she is not.	**RL.4.2**

Amelia Earhart's Last Flight • Practice Test 2

Question & Answer	Standards
1 Part A. This question has two parts. Answer Part A first. Then answer Part B. What is the main idea of the sidebar, "Trying to Solve the Case"? A Science has made great progress in DNA research. B Scientists regard what happened to Amelia Earhart as a detective story. C **Scientists plan to use DNA to match a bone fragment to Amelia Earhart.** D A bone fragment thought to belong to Amelia Earhart may be from a turtle.	**RI.4.2**
1 Part B. Choose two sentences from the sidebar that support the answer to Part A. A Amelia Earhart's plane disappeared over the Pacific in 1937. B All that remained was a mystery—and, on an island near where Earhart disappeared, a bone fragment. C For years there was no way to be sure if this bone was even human. D **But DNA analysis has improved greatly in recent years.** E **It may now be possible to find out if the bone does in fact belong to the famous flyer.** F To determine this, scientists are analyzing a sample of Earhart's saliva.	**RI.4.1**
2 Part A. This question has two parts. Answer Part A first. Then answer Part B. Read the sentence from the passage. If it does, then scientists will test it against the <u>genetic</u> material in the piece of bone. What does the word <u>genetic</u> mean? A made of chemicals B found on an island C taken from a sea turtle D **related to family background**	**RI.4.4**
2 Part B. Which sentence from the sidebar helps you understand the meaning of the word genetic? A The sample came from envelopes that Earhart licked, sealed, and sent many years ago. B No one knows if the sample will yield enough DNA for a proper test. C **They will also compare it with DNA samples from Earhart's living relatives.** D After all, the bone might not be human at all.	**RI.4.4**
3. What structure does the author use to present most of the information in the passage? A **sequence of events** B comparison and contrast C cause and effect D order of importance	**RI.4.5**

Question & Answer	Standards
4. What is the central idea of this passage? A Amelia Earhart was the first woman to fly nonstop across the Atlantic Ocean by herself. B **Amelia Earhart disappeared in 1937 while trying to fly around the world, and no one knows what happened to her.** C Amelia Earhart crossed the Atlantic Ocean as a passenger in 1928, one year after Charles Lindbergh made the first nonstop solo crossing. D Amelia Earhart and Fred Noonan left New Guinea on July 2, 1937, and were never heard from again.	**RI.4.2**
5. How does the author of the passage try to explain Amelia Earhart's disappearance? Check the box next to each sentence. ❑ The U.S. Navy conducted a massive search for Earhart and Noonan that continued for more than two weeks. ❑ **Unable to accept that Earhart had simply disappeared and perished, some of her admirers believed that she was a spy or was captured by enemies of the United States.** ❑ The Navy submitted a report following its search, which included maps of search areas. ❑ Neither the plane nor Earhart nor Noonan were ever found. ❑ **No one knows for sure what happened, but many people believe they got lost and simply ran out of fuel and died.** ❑ Amelia Earhart was less than a month away from her 40th birthday.	**RI.4.8**
6. Choose four sentences that belong in a summary of this passage and put them in correct order. Earhart and her plane disappeared somewhere in the Pacific Ocean, and they were never found. **[3]** Scientists are now analyzing a bone fragment to see if it came from Amelia Earhart. **[4]** Amelia Earhart flew nonstop across the Atlantic Ocean in 1932. **[1]** When Earhart took off from Miami, she left behind some important equipment. In 1937, she and Fred Noonan set off to fly around the world. **[2]** Amelia Earhart became famous for crossing the Atlantic Ocean as a passenger in an airplane.	**RI.4.2**

Question & Answer	Standards
7. Choose three sentences to describe the steps in the process of trying to solve the mystery of what happened to Amelia Earhart. Then put them in correct order. The science of DNA improves over several years. Amelia Earhart's plane vanishes over the Pacific Ocean. Scientists analyze the DNA sample to see if it can be matched to the bone fragment. **[3]** Scientists get a DNA sample of Earhart's saliva from old envelopes. **[2]** Amelia Earhart sends some letters in envelopes. Searchers find a bone fragment on a Pacific Island near the place where Earhart disappeared. **[1]** The U.S. Navy submits a report about its search for Earhart's plane.	**RI.4.3**
8. Why will it be difficult for scientists to prove that the bone fragment came from Amelia Earhart? Give at least two problems the scientists will face. **Sample answer:** The saliva taken from the envelopes might not be enough to yield a good DNA sample, especially since the envelopes are decades old. The bone fragment might not even be human. It was found on a Pacific Island, and it might have come from a sea turtle.	**RI.4.8**
9. How did Amelia Earhart become the "undisputed queen of the air"? Use details from the passage to support your answer. Sample answer: One year after Charles Lindbergh crossed the Atlantic on a solo flight, Earhart became the first woman to fly across the Atlantic as a passenger. In 1932, she became the first woman to make the nonstop solo flight. These two feats made her famous before she decided to fly around the world.	**RI.4.1, RI.4.5**

Question & Answer	Standards
10. Why is it important to find out if the bone fragment found on a Pacific Island came from Amelia Earhart? Use details from the passage to explain. **Sample answer:** The passage refers to Amelia Earhart as "the undisputed queen of the air" and a "famous flyer," so she well known in her day and probably very popular. When she disappeared, people wanted to know what happened to her. The passage says that her admirers could not accept that she had simply disappeared. The mystery has never been solved, and people still want to know what happened. Matching the bone fragment to Earhart would finally provide some answers. It would prove that she died in the Pacific and help determine where it happened.	RI.4.3

Small Rabbit's Long Nap/The Lost Surprise • Practice Test 3

Question & Answer	Standards
1. Read this sentence from the passage "Small Rabbit's Long Nap." All was quiet but for her mother's call, <u>beckoning</u> her home to settle in for winter. Which word means the same as <u>beckoning</u>? A **calling** B asking C moving D sending	**RL.4.4**
2. Why is Small Rabbit afraid when she leaves her family's burrow? A because it is dark B because she is alone C because she becomes lost D **because everything looks different**	**RL.4.3**
3 Part A. This question has two parts. Answer Part A first. Then answer Part B. Which word best describes the white owl? A scary B **caring** C comical D mysterious	**RL.4.3**
3 Part B. Which sentence from the passage best supports the answer to Part A? A "Who, who?" it seemed to ask. "Who, who-who?" B **"Well, Small Rabbit, it's a pleasure to know you. I don't mean to be rude, but I think you must be lost."** C A white owl, much larger than any of the birds she used to know, swooped to a low branch to meet her. D Parting with the owl, Small Rabbit shivered her way back to the burrow; she was cold and wet and sleepy.	**RL.4.1**
4 Part A. This question has two parts. Answer Part A first. Then answer Part B. How does Maria feel after Pablo tells her about what is hidden in the closet? A upset B **excited** C indifferent D disappointed	**RL.4.3**

Question & Answer	Standards
4 Part B. Which line of dialogue from the passage supports the answer to Part A? A "The neighbors will come to the party! And I saw Mama wrapping a big present for you–it's hidden in the hall closet!" B **"Hush, Pablo; it's supposed to be a surprise!" I said, struggling to mask the eagerness in my voice.** C "Patience, Maria. The surprise is the best part." D "What a funny shape!" I whispered, itching with curiosity. "I'll just take a little peek."	**RL.4.1**
5. Which five statements belong in a summary of the passage "The Lost Surprise"? Choose the five sentences and number them in the correct order. Maria had never had her own piñata before. Maria's mother tells her to be patient. **[3]** Pablo tells Maria that he saw their mother wrapping her present. **[1]** Maria decides that next year she will not spoil her birthday surprise. [5] Maria ate pan dulce for breakfast. Maria asks her mother if she can open her present early. **[2]** The piñata was filled with treats. Maria unwraps her present to find out what it is and then rewraps it. **[4]** The piñata was shaped like a horse.	**RL.4.2**
6. Read this sentence from the passage "The Lost Surprise." Practicing my "surprised" face in the mirror, I regretted that I hadn't waited, and that my mother hadn't seen my <u>genuine</u>, delighted reaction. Which word means almost the same thing as <u>genuine</u> as it is used in the passage? A fake B happy C **natural** D surprised	**RL.4.4**
7. If "Small Rabbit's Long Nap" was rewritten as a play, which three elements would be added? Check the box next to each of the elements that you choose. **cast of characters** dialogue stanzas plot **stage directions** verses **scenes or acts**	**RL.4.5**
8. Describe the setting of "Small Rabbit's Long Nap." Use details from the passage to support your answer. **Sample answer:** "Small Rabbit's Long Nap" takes place in a forest. At the beginning of the story, it is autumn. By the end of the story, it is winter. Most of the action in the story takes place out in the forest, outside of Small Rabbit's burrow.	**RI.4.3**

Question & Answer	Standards
9. Compare and contrast how Maria feels at the beginning of the story to how she feels at the end of the story. Use details from the story to support your answer. **Sample answer:** At the beginning of the story, Maria is excited about her birthday. She sneaks a look at her present, and then regrets spoiling her surprise. At the end of the story she is still happy, but decides not to let her impatience affect her in the same way next year.	**RI.4.3, RL.4.1**
10. Both Small Rabbit in "Small Rabbit's Long Nap" and Maria in "The Lost Surprise" make a choice they regret. Compare how these characters respond to their poor choice. Use details from each passage to support your answer. **Sample answer:** Small Rabbit disobeys her mother and goes into the forest while the rest of her family is sleeping. Maria decides to look at her present before her birthday. Both characters regret their decisions. Small Rabbit decides to go back home and sleep with the rest of her family, and is happy when she wakes up in the spring. Maria decides not to spoil her surprise next year, but is not able to fix the mistake she made right away. Both characters learn from their poor choices.	**RL.4.1, RL.4.3, RL.4.9**

A Fire for Liberty/Sybil Ludington's Ride • Practice Test 4

Question & Answer	Standards
1 Part A. This question has two parts. Answer Part A first. Then answer Part B. In the passage "A Fire for Liberty," how did Rebecca Brewton Motte react when the British army made her home, the Brewton House, their headquarters? A She burned the house down. B She moved into a new home. C She decided to support the British cause. D **She continued to aid the American forces.**	**RI.4.1**
1 Part B. Which sentence from the passage supports the answer to Part A? A **She made arrangements to secretly send corn, rice, and pork to the hungry American troops.** B The American troops were on the move toward Charleston, and the British intended to avoid their arrival. C Rebecca spent her days attending to her husband, who was very ill, as well as feeding the British soldiers who were staying in her house. D Not long after, Rebecca's husband died; she then received permission from the British to take her daughters to the family home known as Buckhead, which was outside the city.	**RI.4.3**
2. What is the main idea of the passage "A Fire for Liberty"? A British troops allowed Rebecca Brewton Motte to leave her home after they turned it into a fortress. B The American forces could not have won the Revolutionary War without help from ordinary people. C **Rebecca Brewton Motte made sacrifices to help the American patriots win the Revolutionary War.** D British forces took over the city of Charleston, South Carolina in 1780, but were eventually defeated.	**RI.4.2**

Question & Answer	Standards
3. Choose six sentences that should be included in a summary of "A Fire for Liberty." Number them in the correct order. Rebecca moved with her daughters to her home Buckhead. **[3]** The American patriots asked Rebecca for permission to burn her family's home to get the British out. [5] The British soldiers took over Buckhead and turned it into a fort. **[4]** Rebecca gave Francis Marion the bow that belonged to her brother. The American patriots set fire to the roof of Buckhead and captured the British soldiers. **[6]** The British forces took over the city of Charleston, South Carolina and made their headquarters in Rebecca's home. [1] Rebecca took care of her sick husband. Rebecca secretly sent food to the American soldiers when the British troops were living in her house. **[2]** The British cut down the trees around Rebecca's house and called it Fort Motte.	**RI.4.2**
4. Read this sentence from the passage "Sybil Ludington's Ride." American leaders needed Henry Ludington to <u>muster</u> his volunteer militia to fight the British. Which word means almost the same as <u>muster</u> as it is used in the passage? A help B fight C meet D **gather**	**RI.4.4**
5 Part A. This question has two parts. Answer Part A first. Then answer Part B. According to the passage "Sybil Ludington's Ride," why did Henry Ludington ask his daughter to rally the troops in his place? A He was too tired to go himself. B She was the best horseback rider in town. C **He had to stay and get his farm ready for the militia.** D No one else knew where to find the militia members.	**RI.4.3**
5 Part B. Which paragraph provides support for the answer to Part A? A paragraph 3 B **paragraph 4** C paragraph 5 D paragraph 6	**RI.4.8**

Question & Answer	Standards
6. Choose three details from the passage to support the idea that Sybil Ludington faced many dangers on her ride. Check the box next to each detail you choose. ❏ But there was a problem: the men had disbanded and returned to their farms for the planting season. ❏ They were scattered all over the county. ❏ At 9:00 P.M. that night, rain was falling when she left the family farm. ❏ **Sybil's ride took her on rough roads through rugged countryside and dark woods.** ❏ **She had to watch out for roughnecks and outlaws along the way.** ❏ **She also had to avoid British sympathizers.** ❏ Sybil rode more than forty miles through the night and returned home the next day.	RI.4.3
7. Based on the information presented in the passages, what did Rebecca Brewton Motte and Sybil Ludington have in common? A They both lived in New England. B They both lived with their father. C They both sent food to American troops. D **They both supported the Americans during the American Revolution.**	RI.4.1, RI.4.9
8. Read this sentence from the conclusion of "A Fire for Liberty." Today, Rebecca Brewton Motte is remembered as one of many female patriots who helped the Americans in their struggle for freedom. What evidence does the author present to support this statement? Use details from the passage to support your answer. **Sample answer:** Rebecca Brewton Motte continued to support the American troops even when the British were living in her home. She secretly sent them food. She also allowed the American troops to set fire to her house to get rid of the British. She gave them a bow and arrows to light the fire. <table><tr><td>2</td><td>The response accurately describes how Rebecca Motte helped the Americans during the Revolutionary War and includes at least two details from the passage.</td></tr><tr><td>1</td><td>The response partially describes how Rebecca Motte helped the Americans during the Revolutionary War and includes at least one detail from the passage.</td></tr><tr><td>0</td><td>The response is incomplete or incorrect.</td></tr></table>	RI.4.8

Question & Answer	Standards
9. Read these sentences from the first paragraph of "Sybil Ludington's Ride." Sybil Ludington has been called the "female Paul Revere" and a "Revolutionary War hero." Like Revere, she made a difficult ride on horseback to warn American forces about the approach of British troops. How does the author support the claim that Sybil Ludington's ride was difficult? Use details from the passage to support your answer. **Sample answer:** Sybil Ludingion had to ride forty miles at night through the rain. She had to be careful to stay away from outlaws and people who would turn her in to the British. The ride she took was on rugged paths through dark woods.	**RI.4.8**
10. Compare and contrast the ways that Rebecca Brewton Motte and Sybil Ludington worked to help the American patriots during the Revolutionary War. Use details from the passages to support your answer. **Sample answer:** Both Rebecca Brewton Motte and Sybil Ludington helped the Americans win the Revolutionary War against the British. Rebecca helped the Americans by sending them food. This is something she did more than once. She also let the patriots set fire to the roof of her house when the British were staying there. Sybil also helped the patriots. She put herself in danger to ride around and get together troops to fight the British. According to the passage, she helped the patriots once.	**RI.4.3,** **RI.4.9**